MAGAZINE WRITING FROM THE BOONIES

MAGAZINE WRITING FROM THE BOONIES

BY MARK ZUEHLKE
AND
LOUISE DONNELLY

Carleton University Press
Ottawa, Canada

CARLETON
UNIVERSITY
1942-1992

ISBN 0-8862-9185-2 (paperback)

Printed and bound in Canada

Reprinted 1999

Canadian Cataloguing in Publication Data
Zuehlke, Mark 1955–
Magazine writing from the boonies

1. Authorship.   I. Donnelly, Louise.   II. Title.
Z286.P4D66 1992   808′.02   C92-090476-9

Reprinted by McGILL-QUEEN'S UNIVERSITY PRESS
3430 Mc Tavish Street,
Montreal, P.Q. H3A 1X9

Cover design: Aerographics Ottawa

Acknowledgements :

Carleton University Press gratefully acknowledges the support extended to its publishing programme by the Canada Council and the Ontario Arts Council.

To the Writers and Friends whose

belief helps the writing come easier.

M.Z.

To Terry and Mica S.

L.D.

CONTENTS

INTRODUCTION

No Better Place than Here, Wherever That May Be

Several years ago, a young woman came to one of my spring writing classes and did something surprising. After the class, Louise Donnelly applied what she had learned and sold magazine articles to several regional and national markets before the year's end. Few people taking magazine-writing classes ever do this. Fewer still go from that beginning stage to become seasoned and well-published writers in a mere couple of years. Louise did both and she did it all from the small community of Vernon, which contains no more than 30,000 souls.

This is a community that tops Okanagan Lake in the beautiful, but remote, British Columbia heartland. Virtually no magazines are published in the Okanagan Valley, the economy has always been somewhat flat, and it is a long day's drive from any metropolitan centres. Up until Louise's success in breaking into the magazine industry, I had thought it literally impossible for a writer to thrive in a community stuck out in what is generally considered the boonies.

I had managed to survive and prosper as a magazine writer just down the road from Louise's community in the somewhat larger city of Kelowna (population over 75,000), but had come to think of myself as a bit of an oddity; like a guy who'd heard the party was casual showing up in jeans to face a crowd of tuxedos and formal gowns.

There was I lurking on the fringes of the industry, which at any point might divine the boonie rat I was and close the doors on its formal party to the likes of me forever.

That sounds rather paranoid. It shouldn't. The simple truth is that most successful magazine writers live in metropolitan centres with a healthy, sizeable magazine industry — Toronto, New York, Los Angeles, and the like. Or they live an easy commute away in smaller communities in Connecticut or southern Ontario, where they can get away from the expensive and congested city lifestyle yet still be close to the heartbeat. It all derives from the old economic credo of going where the market is. But what if you are not inclined to do that because you either like where you live or can't simply up and move to the bright lights?

Well, most people give up and, if they continue writing, turn to more freewheeling forms like fiction, or become the neighbourhood columnist for their local newspaper. Both can be rewarding. Unfortunately, as Louise and I have found during our teaching of magazine-writing classes, many of these people remain frustrated and unfulfilled. They want to write for magazines. They want bylines in major national publications. They want to tell true stories in virtually the only medium that allows for this fascinating writing form. They want to write stories about issues and people that probe more deeply than television, radio, or newspapers ever can. They want to make money telling those stories. They also live in the boonies and so feel no one will ever care about what they want or the stories they have to tell.

Louise was the first to twig to this and devised a means of grappling with the problem at a regional level. She created a course entitled "Magazine Writing from the Boonies." It was a brash, unapologetic affirmation of the fact that she was a writer working out of the boonies and was damned proud of it.

I had always walked a quieter line. My courses carry such inspirational titles as "How to Write for Magazines." I could have been in New York for all the title told and looking back on these courses I'm not convinced I addressed adequately the differences in writing from a metropolitan centre and a boonie town.

Boonies? It's at first a word that gets people's backs up. My outdated *Webster's* doesn't even acknowledge it as a word. We all know what it means, though. Especially when we live there. It is an apt description of the bulk of this continent. The boonies are the places out of the mainstream. Off the beaten track. Beyond the power centres of politics, economics, and, in the case of writers, publishing. When we live in the boonies we know it, no matter how often we try not to acknowledge the fact.

Like the country mouse who met the city mouse, we assume those from non-boonie locales are more sophisticated and connected than we are. We go to great lengths to impress them with stories of our local theatre group, symphony, arts community, innovative industries, and anything else that might make our home look less, well, boonieish. We live with an ingrained inferiority complex that dates back at least as far as *Mayberry, RFD (Rural Fire District)*.

When Louise told me what she was going to call her course I had an understandable blip of surprise, even shocked trepidation. Would anyone sign up for a class that so directly tackled the topic which was so much a part of our vague sense of inferiority? Yes. They came the same way writing students always come to such courses. Tentatively. Testing the waters with a delicate toe and wondering whether their talent is sufficient to gain them permission to enter the pool. And when these students come from the boonies they come with a feeling, too, that they might find only room in a wading pool while their big-city brethren hog the pure waters of the Olympic competition pool down the way.

Some come away from our classes (I still don't call mine "Magazine Writing from the Boonies," but only because that's Louise's idea and she deserves all the credit) knowing there is no reason at all why they can't shoulder their way into that Olympic-size pool. All they have to do is work and be professional. No apologizing about where they live, no fear at being a beginner in the magazine industry. For as Louise, myself, and virtually every magazine writer who has come before us or will come along in the future knows, it is not your past or where you live that matters in getting published and making money in this business. What matters is knowing how to write; knowing how to find stories and the markets to sell them to, regardless of where you live.

To this end, Louise and I decided to write this book. It's a book for the boonie rats of North American magazine writing. You may remember that during the Vietnam War, the soldiers who fought in the jungles and did most of the dying were often derisively referred to by those in the rear, who drank cold beer in their air-conditioned offices and talked of body counts, as boonie rats. The funny thing was that the insult became a badge of courage to those in the jungles, and they wore it with pride.

Louise taught me to be like that in a modest way. I now stand up proudly as a boonie writer. I came to it slowly, though, and I can only admire her for always having held her head up high at the front ranks of boonie writerdom.

One final story in this vein before we move on together to the subject of how to make it as a magazine writer from the boonies, the true grit of this book.

Recently, Louise and I travelled to a writers' conference organized by the metropolitan members of the B.C. branch of the Periodical Writers Association of Canada (PWAC). The conference was held in a quaint bed-and-breakfast lodge on an island just a ferry ride away from Vancouver, a city of more than one million people.

For this event the metro writers wore their best country clothes: jeans, bush shirts, running shoes. I almost always wear jeans and running shoes, so I blended in well and was happy enough to do so, having not yet become a self-proclaimed boonie rat writer.

Louise, however, came out on the old lodge porch that morning with a white T-shirt bearing an artful logo in sharp red letters. You probably know what it said: "Magazine Writing from the Boonies."

I swear they all gaped. Why would anyone advertise the fact that she wrote from the boonies? However, as the weekend progressed, they let Louise know she was a magazine writer whose work could proudly stand up alongside the best. A few hours before we caught a ferry to the mainland and began our long trek back home to the boonies, I heard some of these metro writers whispering furtively to Louise that maybe she could get them a shirt like hers. As they slipped away from her I saw a wonderful thing in their eyes. Respect.

Magazine writing from the boonies. It may just be the best place from which to write.

CHAPTER
ONE

Starting Out:
The Quest for Ideas

The first magazine piece I ever sold was to Canada's largest news magazine, *Maclean's*. It was March 1982 and I still vividly remember the editor's assignment phone call. That assignment confirmed that it was possible to write for mass-market national magazines even if I did live in the boonies. As we talked it became clear that not only did the editor not care where I lived but, in this particular case, the article would never have come to be had I not been situated precisely where I was.

You see, the story idea I had proposed to the magazine a few weeks earlier was set in my community, which meant that I was ideally placed to research and write the piece. For too long I had been trying to sell broad theme stories that could have been written by anybody — anywhere — to national magazines, none of which had ever bitten. I tried such topics as a survey of national adoption policies, or an article on the fact that mental health problems are more rampant in rural life than in urban life. (It's true. I have some wonderful research done in New Zealand to prove it.) But the editors were shy to assign an article of such magnitude to an unproven commodity such as myself.

Commodity. An important point to remember. It was when I realized writers are a commodity that I found the path to being published in national magazines. A commodity must have worth, an intrinsic value. The more valuable the commodity, the more desired by the purchaser. A writer's value is directly related to the number and quality of articles he has produced. In 1982 I had hundreds of freelanced daily newspaper articles to my credit, but nary a magazine article. I was a pretty low-value commodity. Had I been an editor, I wouldn't have assigned an article that required any expenses, like travel or long-distance calls, to someone like me. Nor would I have been willing to guarantee any payment through an assignment, but would have preferred such a person to work on speculation.

The trick, then, was to gain value with utmost speed. So I sat down, scrunched my brow, and pondered my backyard. That done, I turned to local newspapers and spent a few days pondering what was going on in the community that would interest a major national magazine. I found it glaring out from the newspaper's front page. The City of Kelowna, through its Chamber of Commerce and several other associations, was throwing a party of appreciation for its local detachment of the Royal Canadian Mounted Police. The boys in red were going to be toasted, wined and dined, and generally hugged and kissed by the people of Kelowna for bestowing upon them their protection.

I sat down and wrote a short query letter (Patience. Louise tells you all about these in Chapter Two.) to *Maclean's* and heard nothing until three days before the banquet. There is a three-hour time difference between Toronto and Kelowna, so I was not at my best when I stumbled from bed to phone at 5:00 A.M. to find a panicky editor on the line. They had misplaced my letter, the editor explained, and only just found it again and could I still take the assignment? Could I go to the banquet? I had a great story. The cops had been taking nothing but abuse the last year or so right across the country and here was this little community saying, "Thank you." Wonderful counterpoint.

It wasn't a big assignment, but it was a start. An enormous meal, interminable speeches, a covey of belly dancers and eighty-seven scarlet red Mounties in one room provided grist for a good story. Two hundred and fifty words later, and "A great night for the Mounties" hit print on April 5, 1982.

It carried the editor's byline first, then "Mark Zuehlken in Kelowna." Even without the misspelling of the name this was not an auspicious beginning.

Still, I could claim publication in *Maclean's* and I did so. From that point on I had gained value as a writer in the business of magazine writing. Seeing the *Maclean's* credential, editors at other magazines, both bigger and smaller, gave me the time of day. They also gave me assignments and picked up expenses.

But it all started from looking around my small world and saying, "What's going on here that matters to others who don't live here?" That's where you start in the magazine-writing business, whether you live in the boonies or a major metropolis. No editor is going to send an untried writer to Lebanon for a piece on sightseeing in a dangerous land, or even give him a long-distance expense account of a couple of hundred dollars to phone up international experts for a thoughtful article on how best to handle nuclear waste. So work with what is at hand: the people, issues, and stories in your community.

Finding Those Stories

But there are no stories here, you whine (I did and sometimes still do). Sure there are. Here are some stories writers from outside Kelowna scooped from under my very nose because I failed to recognize them as nationally interesting. A small boy is mauled by two dogs and a major court case ensues, providing a powerful story for *Reader's Digest*. The Sunshine Theatre Company's talented performances are billed as "a little miracle" in the pages of *Chatelaine*. When a Kelowna houseboat builder manufactured more boats "than the U.S. navy," a writer from several hundred miles away told the story in the Financial Post *Moneywise* magazine because I realized too slowly the company founders' appeal to business publications (I did get on board in time to write for other business magazines on the company's subsequent stunning collapse). Three articles that resulted in major magazine assignments that I never saw but other writers did. So look around. Marketable stories exist everywhere.

Discover these stories by becoming an expert on your community. Read the papers front to back, constantly asking, Is there a story here? Listen to the radio and watch television news. Look behind the news headlines to the story within the story. The small boy being mauled was a story, but what *Reader's Digest* bought was an article that used the boy's experiences as a way of telling parents how to prevent their children from becoming dog-attack victims. That was the real story from the magazine perspective.

Don't just concentrate on the dramatic events in your community. Look closely at the mundane. Louise is great at doing this and I mean no backhanded compliment either, so I'm going to ask her to comment.

Of Dreams and Mundanity

In my first two years of freelancing I sold over fifty stories. Virtually all of them came from my own backyard. Although early in his career Mark had developed a knack for the business story and editors were sending him around the country on assignment, I discovered there were dozens of story ideas within the hundred-mile radius of my rural home.

When it was announced that Vernon would host the first British Columbia Seniors Games (an opportunity for the over-fifty-fives to strut their stuff on the tennis courts, in the swimming pool, and at the cribbage table), I contacted, and eventually sold articles to, four seniors' magazines. I also went on to write a monthly column for one of them covering seniors' events in my area. When a local theatre group won the honour of representing Canadian amateur theatre at a festival in Monaco, I sold the story to a national performing-arts magazine and, later, to a regional lifestyle publication. I sold stories on a local guitar builder to the same lifestyle magazine as well as a national guitar magazine.

Whenever I learn about any community event — a new product someone's developed, a business expansion, or a sports or cultural affair — I immediately ask myself who would buy the story. It's seldom the major national magazines. They require general-interest stories that appeal equally to readers from Victoria to Happy Valley, Labrador. Regional magazines, special-interest publications, and trade journals are likelier markets. Regional magazines look for stories about people, places, and events in their geographical area. Specialty publications focus on specific topics like adventure travel or jewellery making and their stories on white-water rafting or gemstones interest their readers no matter where they live. Trade journals — insider magazines catering to industries and professions — are geared to making their readers richer and smarter. Lawyers subscribe to them. So do plumbers, restaurant owners, and farmers. Trade journals are often receptive to local business stories.

From a small write-up in my community paper I learned that an area printer had undergone a $1 million expansion and bought a state-of-the-art press. I sold this story to a printers' trade journal by sending the newspaper clipping to the editor with a short note asking if he would like an in-depth story geared to his readers. I said I would "not only ask the owners about their new equipment but also how it will improve their bottom line. What type of jobs can they now compete for and how will that affect staffing."

You can work backwards on selling local stories, too. As you're studying the magazines you want to write for, note the type of articles they run and then find suitable stories for them. When I discovered a lifestyle magazine covering the Pacific Northwest with a rural slant that meshed with the area I lived in, I came up with the following proposals — the use of donkeys to guard sheep, the favourite northwest rivers of an international fishing guide, and the struggles of a ginseng grower.

If you have enough imagination and energy, you can sell just about any story in your community. The smaller markets often pay well for the time invested and the major markets you break into add heft to your résumé, perhaps enough for you to tackle stories outside your area. Meanwhile, editors recognize you as a writer — often the only writer in the area

— and count on you for regional coverage. Just one of the advantages of writing from the boonies.

Back to you, Mark.

Creative Eavesdropping

One often-neglected source of magazine articles is conversation. Think of how often people tell you something interesting, something you never thought of before, or something common to us all but seldom examined in depth. In these conversations are found ideas.

A few years back a friend was telling me his financial troubles. Self-employed, he had trouble convincing bank managers to risk giving him a loan. Realizing this is a dilemma every self-employed person faces, I phoned an editor at the Financial Post *Moneywise* magazine and won an assignment. I used my own experiences, those of my friend, and several other local self-employed people as the jumping-off point. Then I threw in comments from local accountants and bank managers on what they want to see from self-employed people and how to make the process less painful. "The Loan Arranger Writes Again" became a major article in one of the nation's leading financial magazines. All because I listened to a friend and saw a potential article in his words.

So, in the beginning concentrate on your community as the source for cheaply researched and easily written articles. Think of this time as an internship in the profession of magazine writing. And like an intern you soon reach a level of skill, competence, and status that encourages editors to assign you articles set in locales beyond your community.

The time you spend doing only local articles can be amazingly short. It all depends on how quickly you grow as a magazine writer and, as in all things, on luck. I had luck on my side. After the *Maclean's* article my second major national article was for what was then, and is now again, called *The Financial Post Magazine*. It was a local story, but this time it was a major feature of 3,500 words. The editor I was working with liked the article and asked me to send her more story ideas. Taking advantage of such encouragement, I asked her if I could look at stories outside my region. Certainly, she said, and I immediately did.

A major feature-article assignment followed on the unique costs and lifestyle choices faced by residents of Canada's most northerly city, Whitehorse, in Yukon Territory. There were writers in Whitehorse who could have done this story, but I saw the article idea and they didn't. So it was mine. Two weeks in Whitehorse, more than $1,000 in expenses later, and I had a 3,500-word feature in one of Canada's top magazines and $1,600 in my pocket for the effort.

Since then, I have travelled to numerous communities across western Canada to do stories for this and other publications. Once you reach this stage there are few disadvantages in writing from the boonies. You, too, can travel as well as anyone in a major city. All that's needed is the ability to get on a plane, board a train, or drive a car and you're away.

You can even get assignments taking you to the major urban centers to write stories the locals missed. A few years back a short newspaper item reported that West Vancouver, a chic suburb across the Lion's Gate Bridge from Vancouver, contained the highest per capita income earners in Canada. I knew *Moneywise* would love a story about these people — how much they earned, how they earned it, how they spent it, what their homes were like, what their community was like, what their dreams were. My editor there snapped it up and I spent more than a week walking the streets of West Vancouver and talking to people to put together another major feature. There are Vancouver writers I know who still wonder how they missed that story opportunity. The answer, of course, is that they had never learned to do what a boonie writer must do to survive: constantly look at everything around you and ask if a story lurks there.

Don't Forget That Long-Distance Feeling

Once editors are willing to fork out expense money, there is an even easier way to research stories outside your community than by travelling. The telephone becomes an important writing tool. With it you can talk to the world's leading authority on franchise business sales, chat with a famous country singer about his life and times, or interview a prima ballerina about her collection of wooden decoy ducks. With the telephone, you no longer live in an isolated location. You are suddenly in the very thick of things.

Having established your competence by writing about local stories, you will have little trouble getting editors at major national magazines to foot a few phone calls. In fact, being in the boonies is actually an asset when doing phone research. Too many of my colleagues living and writing in major cities are disinclined to put up with the bother of long-distance calls to other parts of the country or continent in assembling their research material. There is usually an expert to be found locally, they reason, so if the expert is not the leader in a field, what does it matter? But from where I live all the experts are a long-distance call away, so why not shoot for the top person in the field? Why not conduct interviews with people across the country on your subject? This gives the story a national feel and makes it relevant to the readers no matter where they live. The telephone gives you the ability to conduct research and collect a story covering a national issue, whether it be how to buy rental real estate or invest in penny stocks.

The key to attaining such flexibility in the articles you write rests on establishing yourself in the minds of editors as a seasoned professional. To do that you need, from the beginning, to approach editors correctly. They don't care what your past education is, where you live, or what you wear while you write. They care only that you are a professional in the magazine industry. So how do you approach them to demonstrate this professionalism at the very outset? It's simple, really, and Louise explains it all in the next chapter.

CHAPTER TWO

Dear Magazine Editor:
How to Sell Ideas

When I took Mark's one-day magazine writing class, I had no idea what a query letter was. I assumed you thought up a story, researched it, wrote it, sent it off to the magazine, and, shortly after, received either a cheque or a rejection slip. So I was delighted when Mark told us you wrote a query letter first. Simply, a query letter is a pitch to the editor stating your idea, its suitability for the magazine, and your qualifications for writing the article.

Sounds easy, right? Well, it can be, but I discovered queries are often more difficult to write than the article itself. Yet a good query letter is your best sales tool. It lets editors decide quickly whether the story is for them and then allows them to expand or adjust the focus of your story before you go to the trouble of writing an article. A query also forces you to narrow down your topic and get a handle on the slant, and sometimes even provides the article's lead. More about that later.

Choosing a Market

First, determine a potential market for your query. By now, you've taken to checking out the magazines in your dentist's office, nagging friends for back issues of their subscriptions, and surreptitiously reading copies of new magazines at the newsstand. There're a lot of magazines out there. The Canadian Magazine Publishers Association estimates there are 5,000 periodicals published in Canada including trade journals, consumer magazines, and newsletters. *Writer's Market*, a directory of North American markets, lists 4,000 places to sell your work, including hundreds of magazines. So how do you choose the right magazine for your story idea?

Say you hear of someone in the next town who's invented a device to make tying a tie easier. You know — first you tie it too long — then too short. So this guy develops a permanent stick-on dot to mark the place where the short end of the tie crosses over the long end. He also has the marketing savvy to call his product "Knot Dot." (I once tried to sell a story on something with the explicit but unsexy name, Automatic Residential Stovetop Fire Extinguisher.) The slightly off-beat nature of this story appeals, so you phone for a short interview, just enough to write your query letter. Remember, right now you're still paying for long-distance phone calls, although if you make a sale, most editors will reimburse expenses. (We discuss expenses in the next chapter and Mark gives you the low-down on economical research in Chapter Four.)

Talking to the inventor, you decide this would be a great story for a business magazine. After all, you reason cagily, businessmen wear ties and their time's precious, so they would welcome learning about something that could help them knot ties more quickly. If you're not already aware of various financial magazines, now is the time to drop around the library and look through *Writer's Market* or other magazine directories. While you're there, glance through the periodical indexes to see if the story has already been done. Periodical indexes such as *Reader's Guide To Periodical Literature* or *Canadian Periodical Index* list published articles by topic, author, and magazine. From talking to the inventor you know he hasn't received any press yet, but the periodical indexes might turn up a business publication you didn't know about.

Soon you have a dozen financial publications listed. Then it hits you: perhaps there's a trade journal for tie retailers. Or what about the grooming section of men's magazines? Perhaps a farm paper might be interested. Their readers may seldom wear ties, but that could be the hook — since they have so little experience with ties, they may need all the help they can get. Or perhaps during the interview you discovered the inventor belongs to a service club. Wouldn't the club's newsletter love to hear what one of its members is doing in his spare time? Amazed, you total up eighteen possible magazines.

Before you dash home to whip off eighteen query letters, we need to discuss the thorny issue of multiple, or simultaneous, submissions. This is where you submit the same story idea to more than one magazine at the same time. For the writer, this is great. It increases the chances of making a sale and greatly reduces the time it takes to make that sale. If you send out a single query and wait an average of eight weeks to receive a reply, you're limited to approaching only six markets in a year. And by the end of that year, the story may no longer be valid. And this problem is truly compounded with seasonal or timely stories.

But simultaneous submissions alienate many editors. They feel if they take the time to consider your query, you should extend them the courtesy of an exclusive submission. There are exceptions. Many religious publications don't mind simultaneous submissions because they have non-competing readerships. It's not likely that a Catholic also subscribes to a Baptist publication. Occasionally, other magazines are listed in market directories as accepting simultaneous submissions as long as you identify your query as such. But, you probably worry, such an admission skews your chances of an acceptance. Here's what I do.

First, it's all right to send out queries on our inventor to a financial magazine, a trade journal, a farm paper, and a club publication at the same time. I would be writing different stories for each of them and they're not likely to have a competing readership. These spin-offs — different stories using much the same research — are the best way to maximize profits. By asking a few extra questions during the interview, I'd have all the information I needed for the various magazines.

Secondly, for a time-sensitive story I state a deadline in my query. Something like, "Due to the timely nature of this story, if I don't hear from you within two weeks I will have to withdraw my submission."

I haven't yet sent out simultaneous submissions to competing magazines. I try, though, to generate sales by querying on as many spin-off ideas as possible. In her excellent book *How To Write Irresistible Query Letters* (Writer's Digest, 1987), Lisa Collier Cool defends simultaneous submissions and says that although she's never had two markets wanting the same story in her thirteen-year career, if it did happen she "would sell to the highest bidder and decline the other offer." Rather than refusing to buy future articles, she adds, the rejected editor is even more eager to buy, the next time around. Of course, as a contributing editor to *Cosmopolitan* and with *Glamour*, *Playgirl*, *Family Circle*, and *Harper's* credits, she's got the clout to back up her decision.

No doubt simultaneous submissions will eventually be accepted practice. But meanwhile, if you're hesitant, increase your chances of making a sale with spin-off ideas.

Decoding the Masthead

Now that you've targeted your magazines, to whom should you send your query? Turn to the front of the magazine and within the first couple of pages you find the masthead, a list of the people who work at the magazine. Managing editor is your best bet or articles editor if there's a large staff. Seldom would you query the publisher or the executive editor. They have very little to do with assigning work. Of course, a small magazine may list only an editor and an art director, so then the choice is easy. You may occasionally see a listing for contributing editor. This could strike you as the person to contact — after all, you do want to contribute a story. But contributing editors are just are lucky freelancers who contribute to the magazine on such a regular basis that they've been given a title.

If I'm studying an outdated magazine (more than a year old) or an older market directory, I spring for a short phone call to the magazine's receptionist (the telephone number is often listed in the masthead) to confirm that the editor is still with the magazine. You look something less than professional if you send a query addressed to an editor who left the magazine nine months ago. Of course, this applies only to magazines which are not readily available at newsstands. When you query a major magazine, you'll have read the current issue as well as countless back issues. Right?

Near the bottom of the masthead is the magazine's editorial address, usually preceded by the phrase, "Such and Such Magazine is published twelve times a year by ABC Company." This is where you send your query letter and, later, your completed manuscript. (Don't confuse this with the advertising office address, usually noted as such. Magazines often have one or more of these offices which sell ad space and have nothing to do with the editorial side of the business.)

It's helpful to know how often the magazine is published. It could be monthly or quarterly, or it could have an unusual schedule like eight or ten times a year. Some magazines combine two months into one issue during their slow advertising periods. Take note of your particular market's schedule. If your idea is best suited to a specific issue, begin submitting your query six to eight months in advance. This allows time for possible rejections before making a sale.

A query suggesting a story for a summer issue, perhaps "Surviving the Family Vacation," should go out no later than mid-January. Most magazines finalize editorial line-up at least two months before the printing deadline. A July issue would be printed in early June with most articles assigned by April. For submissions geared to annual celebrations like Christmas or April Fool's Day, it's not too early to start querying a year ahead.

Selling Your Story

I try to keep my query letters to one page, using a couple of paragraphs to sell the story, a line or two to ask for the sale, and another paragraph to describe my qualifications. I also state whether I can provide photographs (often a requirement with small magazines; major magazines assign professional photographers to illustrate stories). If the query runs longer than a page, I often attach my qualifications separately, in the form of a brief résumé.

Perhaps now is a good time to mention that I made my first sale without a query letter. I submitted a 500-word piece to a regional business magazine. The editor phoned to tell me the piece wasn't for her, but she liked my writing style and invited me to drop by her office with more ideas when I was in town. Now, this doesn't happen often to boonie writers as there are so few magazines published in the smaller areas. But when it does, do your homework. Using the guidelines from the previous chapter, make a list of appropriate stories and go to your meeting prepared to come away with an assignment. Editors are busy people. If they ask you to drop by, they're interested in giving you work.

I pitched several story ideas to the editor, came away with three or four assignments, and continued to write regularly for the magazine for the next year. Its low fees eventually forced me to abandon it for more lucrative markets, but that first sale made up for the pile of rejection letters I had accumulated.

Those rejection letters, however, were encouraging. I sent out dozens of query letters during the five months it took to make that first sale. The personal notes I was getting back (no form rejection slips yet) told me I was getting close. Sometimes my timing was off (the magazine was already planning a similar story), or I had misread their readership. I still got the occasional "Thanks for the query on tattoos, but I don't think it's the sort of thing for us." But when I discovered the following story, I knew I had a winner.

If you look at Sample Letter 1, you can see the query that tied up my first sale to a major national publication.

Yes, there really is a Knot Dot. You didn't think I was clever enough to make it up, did you? (I also wasn't clever enough to spin the story idea off to all the markets I came up with when writing this chapter.) For months I had tried to break into *Moneywise*, so I had only one publication in mind when I heard about the Knot Dot. I felt the story was perfect for its front section on new trends, businesses, and products.

My address/date

Susan Grimbly
Managing Editor
The Financial Post *Moneywise* Magazine

Dear Ms. Grimbly,

What's this?

It's a Knot Dot.
Knot Dot is the brainchild of a Kelowna, British Columbia entrepreneur. Andy Heredy, an engineer, was frustrated by the time it took to knot his tie to the correct length.

When his Canada-wide search failed to turn up any sort of device to help him, he decided to invent something himself.

Is *Moneywise* interested in 500 words for Starting Post on this dotty solution to a knotty problem?

I write regularly for the regional magazine *Okanagan Business*.

I look forward to hearing from you.

Sincerely,

Louise Donnelly

SAMPLE LETTER 1

Having read dozens of back issues, I knew the editor liked a sassy approach to this section and wasn't above a little word play. I stuck a blue Knot Dot under "What's this?" and popped the query in the mail. Ten days later I had a firm assignment.

These front sections (occasionally they're in the back of the magazine), which feature a collection of short, snappy stories are a good place to break into a magazine if you have little or no experience. The editors don't have a lot of space to fill, so are likelier to risk working with an inexperienced writer.

Here's another successful query (see Sample Letter 2), this one for Canadian Airlines' inflight magazine, *Canadian*.

My address/date

Leslie Johnson
Editor/*Canadian*

Dear Ms. Johnson,

When Lyn Van Dov watched her first Ironman Triathlon on television she was overwhelmed by the spectacle of athletes pushing themselves beyond the imagined limits of endurance — a 2.4-mile (4 km) swim followed by a 112-mile (180 km) cycle and then a full 26.2-mile (42 km) marathon.

Since then, Van Dov herself has run a triathlon of sorts. First she plunged into uncharted water as race director for the first Ironman Canada Triathlon in 1986. Then she peddled like crazy supporting the annual August event through a non-profit society. Finally, this past December, when the society hit the wall with financial difficulties, she bought Ironman Canada herself.

While her new company, Next Age Development, will run the Penticton, B.C.-based Ironman Canada (one of only five Ironman races in the world) as a business, she uses her background in radio and film production to bring a theatrical quality to this "inner sport. Ironman is so wholesome, so important and so positive, it's a very special phenomenon. Race-day is a one-day passion play," she says.

Is *Canadian* interested in a profile on this guru of the ultimate new age sport?

I'm sorry you couldn't use the story on the Western Artist Group but I look forward to working with you on this one.

Sincerely,

Louise Donnelly

Writing sample enclosed.

SAMPLE LETTER 2

There are a few points about Louise's queries that deserve closer examination, so I'm going to interrupt for a moment. Query writing, as you see from her examples, gives the editor a story idea, demonstrates the writer's talent, and does all this without consuming a lot of the editor's precious time.

A delicate balance must be struck. Attaining this balance is what makes the writing of queries such a challenge.

So how did Louise do? Let's look at Knot Dot first. Here, Louise had luck on her side. Not too often can you bundle up the subject of your article and send it along with your query. (What's this? A nuclear submarine.) But when you get a chance like this, take it. That opening line, combined with the visual and tactile presence of the Knot Dot, was guaranteed to capture Susan Grimbly's attention.

In the next two paragraphs Louise gives the editor everything she needs to know about the product and its inventor. Forty-nine words. That's brevity.

The following sentence proposes a word guideline and where the piece would fit nicely into the magazine. More importantly, it is where Louise displays the fact that she can write in a manner that transcends mere technical proficiency: "this dotty solution to a knotty problem?" *Moneywise* editors love word play and Louise shows them she knows that and can play the game too.

The following paragraph simply tells the editor Louise isn't a totally new kid on the writing block. Yet it also shows that she is not a seasoned resident. Editors like to know where you are in the business when they hear from you. And it's not so they can ignore new writers in favour of the older hands. Editors are always looking for new blood, new talent; it's what keeps the industry alive and vital.

To Susan Grimbly, Louise was a new kid on the national-magazine street. A new kid with enough talent and creativity to warrant a crack at an assigned piece. The piece was brief, so if Louise fell short, the magazines's risk was minimal.

The Van Dov query is more typical of what most writers have to deal with when presenting a story idea. Van Dov wouldn't fit in an envelope, so words alone would make or lose the sale. Again, however, watch how Louise captures the editor's interest.

At the outset we are drawn tightly into Van Dov's passion for Ironman triathlons. In the first two paragraphs we see a woman, initially entranced by a television event, become the driving force of one of only five such races in the world.

More importantly, look at the language. There are three images in the second paragraph, one for each leg of a triathlon: Van Dov "plunged into uncharted waters"; "peddled like crazy"; "the society hit the wall." Swimming, biking, and the ultimate running endurance crisis of hitting the wall are all metaphorically wedded to Van Dov's own struggles to create the Ironman contest. That is good writing. Good writing in the tight, concise framework of a query. Good writing guaranteed to capture an editor's attention.

The final paragraphs give the details the editor needs to decide whether Van Dov's story is sufficiently interesting to airline readers, asks for the sale, and reminds the editor that Louise has knocked on the magazine's door before. Most editors appreciate a promising writer who has the tenacity to keep trying to break into their publications.

Two good queries. I agree with Louise, by the way, when she says queries are tough to write. It takes time to string together a tight paragraph that is vividly written and that also conveys the information the editor needs to justify an assignment. There are no easy formulas. Each query must be crafted around the subject it concerns. Some run longer than these examples, some may be even shorter. The subject tends to play the tune.

The Phone Excuse

I'm taking up a bit more of Louise's chapter to tell you that, luckily, there are times when you don't have to write a query (or pitch an idea in person) to get an assignment. After selling several articles to a publication, I usually stop writing queries and instead phone the editor with my ideas. The advantages are that I get an answer more quickly, I avoid pitching ideas to editors who already have something similar in the works, and I am sometimes able to shape an idea more precisely to their needs during the conversation. Usually, if they want the piece, they ask for a short outline setting out enough information for them to take into an editorial story meeting. These are really just notes on the subject matter and don't need to be as carefully constructed as the query.

There is a drawback to phone proposals. When you live in the boonies, as we do, it can be expensive and so isn't really advisable unless you think the idea is a sure bet. The other thing is that you have less control over a phone conversation than a query letter. If you feel depressed, bored, or disinterested that day, it may be hard to sell an editor on anything. So, even when you've reached the stage where phone queries are acceptable to an editor, don't phone if you're not in a mood to be enthusiastic about your story idea.

Think Slant, Not Subject

This is Louise again. Remember at the start of this chapter I said your query could help define your topic and its slant and sometimes provide the lead. You may find, when you first start writing, that while you have a subject, you don't know what aspect of that subject you should offer to write about. Hoping the editor will narrow down the topic, you may be tempted to send off a vague, generalized query. Don't.

Magazines keep a "picture" in their editorial minds of their readers. This picture is composed of the readers' interests and values, their social, educational, and economic backgrounds, and the magazine's perception of its own agenda, style, and taboos. The editor's job is to match articles to the picture, providing readers with the information and entertainment they expect.

Sometimes this picture is compared to the "window" a space shuttle must pass through on its return to earth. If it comes in too high, it bounces back into space; too low, and it burns up. To survive, your story idea, like the shutle, must be right on target.

Take time to tailor your query to its market. In doing so, you trim that too-big subject down to a close fit for a particular magazine. (I won't say perfect fit because editors can, and do, reject even the most seasoned writer's ideas if they are not for them.) A magazine's cover lines tell you a lot about the stories it's looking for. Cover lines are the blurbs on the front cover: "The Thinking Woman's Sport"; "10 Flowers That Bloom after Dark"; "Sell Your First Story."

Careful scrutiny of these cover lines, and even the advertising inside, helps you discern the difference between a magazine and its competitors. Address this difference, often called the magazine's slant, and your query will likely be considered.

Take the popular home-renovation market. One magazine's cover lines read, "Make Your Own Victorian Screendoor"; "Renovate Your Kitchen in Five Week-ends"; "Easy Wall Finishes." Another says, "Choose the Best Interior Designer"; "Trail Blazing Architects"; "Working with Your Landscaper." It's easy to see that one magazine is for the do-it-yourselfer, while the other caters to an upscale readership that prefers to hire professionals for renovations. A quick look at the advertising confirms this. One has ads for lots of do-it-yourself products; the other, ads for services and consultants.

Your subject may be "faux finishes," using paint to mimic marble, tortoiseshell, granite, and other expensive surfaces. This subject could fill books, and does. Narrow it down to contemporary wall finishes and you have an article-size topic. (Be choosy with the information you provide or even this idea could swell up to booksize.) If your slant is "Four Faux Finishes for Beginners," try the do-it-yourself magazine. "Top Faux Finish Artists" would be better with the upscale magazine.

I knew I wanted to write about Ironman Canada, not because I'm athletic or knowledgeable about sports, but because Penticton is within driving distance of my home and we boonie writers can't let any topic escape us, especially if we can sell it to a national magazine. But I didn't have a slant yet.

I had decided that *Canadian*'s readers, mostly business travellers, would be intrigued by Ironman Canada's dynamic founder and her determination to run the race as a business, so I narrowed my story idea down to Van Dov. She became the focus of my query. And when I initially interviewed Van Dov by phone, her perception of the gruelling event gave me the slant (and eventual title) for my story — "Ironman: The New Age Sport."

Preparing my query forced me to define the one aspect of the Ironman triathlons I would try to sell to *Canadian*'s editor and to come up with a slant compatible with the magazine's needs. Most airline in-flight magazines want upbeat contemporary stories and I felt "New Age" conveyed those qualities.

Finally, even though I didn't use the query's first two paragraphs as my article lead, I was able to incorporate them into the story.

It turned out that, rather than a profile, the editor wanted the piece tailored to a fitness column and asked me to concentrate on Ironman's appeal to both the athletes and Van Dov. Needless to say, it's important to give editors what they want. I'll go into greater detail about this in the next chapter.

Sell Yourself, Too

You notice the only qualification I mentioned in the Knot Dot query was that I wrote for a regional publication. I had very few writing credits at that point but I hoped my idea, rather than my experience, would get me the assignment. By the time I wrote the Ironman query I had a better résumé and could mention several magazines I had written for. Since I had recently queried the same editor (and been turned down) about an artists' group and included photocopies of published work, I didn't need to list my qualifications again, but I did remind her of our previous correspondence, and I enclosed a current writing sample.

In the beginning, your résumé may be pretty slim, too. But don't be discouraged. Often your best qualification is simply living where the story takes place. And you may have other qualifications, too. If you're proposing a story on rock climbing and you're an avid rock climber, mention that. If you and your six kids take a camper across the country every summer, you may be just the person to write about travelling with children. If your job gives you access to information that is not available to the general public, say so. Something like "As a professional escort, I can provide fourteen tips for surviving a blind date" is bound to impress an editor.

On the other hand, don't draw attention to your inexperience by mentioning that you have no published credits. The editor probably realizes that; why make it obvious? Always present yourself in the best light, without stretching the truth. Be positive. Enthusiastic. Professional.

All queries should be typed (or computer-printed) in black on good-quality white bond. No fancy type, no coloured ink, and no coloured paper. Whatever equipment you use, just make sure the print is dark, clear, and easy to read. And include a self-addressed stamped envelope (SASE) for the editor's reply. Without this, you may never hear back from the magazine at all. I still enclose a SASE with all my queries, even to magazines I write for regularly. Editors appreciate not having to take the time to address an envelope and I think it speeds their reply.

Still, I don't think any writer ever feels the replies come back quickly enough. So how long should you wait to hear from a magazine? Generally, I wait about six to eight weeks (I know, it seems like forever) and then I send off a little note asking whether the editor has had a chance to make a decision yet. I also work in any new information that might tip the scales my way. I wait one more month, then I send the query to another market. You may also write and let the first magazine know you're withdrawing the story. I don't usually bother. If they haven't got back to you by then, they're probably not interested.

To recap this long chapter, remember: Write the strongest query you can. Make it neat, sharp, and to the point, and mail it off with a SASE. Then sit down and write some more. The more queries you have out there, the more work you pick up. And the happiest writers I know are the ones with work stacked higher than their file cabinets.

CHAPTER
THREE

The Gentle Art of Negotiation

Mark and I joke that he is "laid-back" about writing while I have a "driven approach." If work is going badly or, worse yet, there is no work, Mark stretches out with a good book. I, on the other hand, spend my time writing away for sample copies of magazines, searching through my idea file for another story, or just plain worrying. Both of us, though, are disciplined in our own ways and keep the assignments coming. We don't lose sight of our goal to earn a living from our writing.

Freelancing is a precarious existence at best, so hone your bargaining skills from the start. As new writers, be prepared for those first acceptances. Whether they come by mail or by phone, take a deep breath, promise yourself you'll celebrate later, and then coolly negotiate the best assignment you can.

All professional writers (feel free to call yourself a pro from the moment you commit your integrity, effort, and ability to writing for money) are concerned with content, length, deadline, rights, expenses, and payment. Before accepting an assignment, make sure you and your editor agree on all these points.

Know Your Rights

Our productivity largely determines our income. The more we write, the more we earn. The only restriction, aside from lack of marketable ideas, is time. There are only so many writing

29

hours available in a day. If we are resourceful enough to write two or three major articles a month, we could gross perhaps $20,000 to $30,000 annually. Some writers who consistently write for top-paying markets earn much more. Some, including myself, earn less. Aside from moving into the better-paying markets, which we should strive to do, the only means to increase our magazine-writing income is to negotiate higher fees (more on that later) or re-sell what we've previously written. To do this, we must retain copyright and as many publishing rights to our work as possible.

Copyright, says the *Writer's Encyclopedia* (Writer's Digest, 1986), is "a proprietary right designed to give the creator of a work the power to control that work's reproduction, distribution, and public display or performance, as well as its adaption to other forms." In other words, we're talking ownership. In Canada and the United States, an artist's work (writing, in our case) is deemed to belong to its creator.

When we retain copyright, rather than selling our article, we grant the magazine a licence to publish our work. Most major magazines are only concerned with *first serial rights*. This is the right to be the first publication in a geographical area to print your article. A Canadian magazine usually requests first Canadian serial rights (meaning that it will be the first to publish your article in Canada) while an American magazine may ask for first North American serial rights (the right to be the first in North America to publish the article). American magazines are so widely distributed in Canada that most U.S. publishers don't want your story appearing in a Canadian periodical at the same time. (Please note that, when discussing publishing rights, the word "serial" means magazine or periodical and doesn't imply an ongoing situation.)

In Canada, you may want to specify first Canadian serial rights in language of origin if the magazine publishes an English and a French version. This way you could negotiate an additional fee if the magazine chooses to have your work translated for use in its sister publication. (In publications such as in-flight magazines where your work appears in both

English and French in the same issue, there is no additional payment.)

You might also consider adding a time limit to those first serial rights, something like, "until publication or for twelve (or twenty-four, or whatever) months — whichever is sooner." This discourages a magazine from accepting your story and then delaying publication unduly, preventing you from marketing second serial rights.

The sale of *second serial rights* (also called reprint rights) allows writers to make additional income marketing work they've previously published. Many smaller magazines are interested in second rights. A regional lifestyle magazine may take the profile of a local artist you managed to sell to a national publication. Perhaps a dozen or more trade publications might be interested in reprinting your advice on reducing staff sick-days. Mark gives details on selling and submitting your work the second time around, in Chapter Eight.

You can continue to re-sell your published work as long as you can scare up a buyer. Simply let the magazine know it's purchasing second rights, not first rights. And as you continue to re-sell your work, note that it's always called *second* serial rights, not third or fourth rights.

A writer can also increase the income for an article by selling simultaneous rights. This is where the same story is sold to two or more publishers at the same time. These publishers are most likely in different geographic areas with non-competing readers. A good example is selling a travel piece to several newspapers across the country. Do ensure that none of the papers is a national paper, distributed across the country, such as *The Globe and Mail*. Mark your queries or manuscripts with "exclusive your territory," to let the editors know you're not submitting the same idea or story to a competitor in their trading area.

Be wary of selling *all* rights. Once you sell all rights to a particular work, you can never market it again. Therefore, any fee negotiated for all rights must be generous. Also, any writing done under a work-for-hire agreement belongs to your employer, not you.

There are other rights such as television or movie rights, and while few magazine writers have their work performed, we should be aware of these rights. You never know, someone might want to make your award-winning environmental article into a documentary. Be cautious and know what you're selling. Take every opportunity to increase your understanding of copyright law. It only strengthens your bargaining power.

When I started writing I knew very little about publishing rights. Editors never asked for specific rights and I didn't offer any. After awhile, I worried that with this casual attitude, I might have lost all rights to my published articles. I contacted the Canadian Copyright Institute in Toronto. After several months, they wrote reassuringly that they had sought legal advice to answer my question: where no rights are specified, they said, upon publication all rights revert back to the author. Still, it's in your best interest to clarify which rights the magazine is buying.

Words Count

Always ask the editor for the approximate length of your proposed article. It is usually given as a word count. Up-front pieces run to around 350 to 500 words, a short feature 1,200 to 1,500 words, and a major article 2,500 to 5,000 words. You can calculate the length of a published piece if you know there are approximately 1,000 words on an average $8\frac{1}{2}$-by-11-inch magazine page without photographs. In the beginning, I actually counted magazine articles word by word to determine the average length of the shorter stories.

I was afraid I would be assigned a 4,000-word story without having the research or writing skills to produce a tightly crafted piece. I need not have worried. Seldom did the topics I proposed at that time lend themselves to in-depth journalism and gradually I developed the confidence to handle longer assignments. Most new writers could competently write a 1,200-word story. That's only five double-spaced manuscript pages.

In my one-day workshop on magazine writing, I'm often asked whether a writer must meet the word count exactly. There is some leeway, perhaps 25 to 50 words on a 1,200-word piece and 150 words on a longer story. It's actually better to be a little short than too long. There is a finite amount of magazine space allotted to an editor, so if your piece is too long, it must be cut to fit.

Inexperienced editors occasionally tell you to write the story as long as it has to be. If this happens, check the usual length of the magazine's articles and write accordingly. Otherwise, you're likely to have your story ruthlessly slashed to fit its assigned pages. The practicalities of the magazine industry always take precedent over "art."

For those who use their computer's word count, one last caution. A computer only counts actual words and doesn't take into account the space at the end of short lines or paragraphs. Relying on your computer's word count can make your piece 20 percent longer than it should be. The authors of *Word Processing Secrets for Writers* (Writer's Digest, 1989) recommend that you divide the total number of characters by five for an accurate count.

What Do You Want?

When you negotiate an assignment, make sure you and the editor agree on the article's slant. Until you begin your in-depth research you won't always know the whole story. However, understand what the editor expects to receive; if it looks like the story is taking a different turn, call up to clarify the situation. Editors don't appreciate surprises (except perhaps on their birthdays).

During your negotiations, ask what information is crucial to the story. If you're doing a piece on a local kitchen designer for a trade journal specializing in the residential kitchen market, let the editor know you plan to discuss market trends, popular designs, and tips for increasing sales. This shows that you're aware of the expectations of the magazine's readers. You may be asked to include interviews with one of the designer's clients and perhaps a retailer or two. The editor might also give you inside information on the industry, say, a revolutionary countertop that's just hitting the market, and want you to question the designer on its potential. Again, give editors what they want, and when you can't, let them know.

Money, Money, Money

Now we're up to the big question: how much are you going to get paid? And just as important, when are you going to get paid? Many new writers don't know there are two policies for paying writers, one good and one bad.

Let's start with the bad one. It's called payment on publication. This means you won't see one red cent until the magazine publishes your article. You could submit your story in early January, two weeks later hear from the editor that it's fine, then wait until October for publication, and finally receive a cheque in late December. And that's not the worst that can happen.

The magazine could change its editorial direction, a new editor may not like your work, or the magazine could acquire new owners or even fold. If the result is that your story isn't published, you won't be paid at all. This is a worst-case scenario, but even at its best, payment on publication means the money is in the publisher's bank account when it could be in yours.

Magazines rely on the profits generated by their advertising sales to provide the cash to pay their expenses, including writer fees. I can understand (although I don't like it) a new magazine resorting to a payment-on-publication policy until it's on its feet, but there's no excuse for established magazines. They shouldn't be looking to writers to subsidize their business venture. We take a risk writing for these magazines and, as soon as we can, we should move on to better markets.

The best deal for a writer is payment on acceptance. This means that once an editor is satisfied with your story and accepts it, he sends your invoice (which you cunningly enclosed with your manuscript) to the accounting department. Within thirty days you should have the cheque in hand.

Most magazines have standard rates for freelance writing. Usually quoted on a per-word basis, these fees can run from one or two cents to well over a dollar per word. I don't recommend that anyone should write for mere pennies a word, but I never turn down work solely on the basis of the per-word rate.

If the magazine offers at least twenty cents a word I consider the assignment. If it's a story I want to do and can research and write in a reasonable length of time, I take it. I always look at the time involved rather than just the fee. A $400 story I can complete in two working days (five hours for research and interviews and ten hours for writing and then polishing the final draft) is acceptable to me.

You might also consider a low-rate assignment for other reasons. If you spin off a story on information you already have, your time-to-effort ratio is still good. You may want to write the story or work for a particular magazine. New writers or boonie writers like us may choose not to pass up any writing opportunity within reason. We have to look at this period in our careers as an apprenticeship. While we work for low rates, we're gaining experience and building a solid résumé. However, by no means am I suggesting we stay in this position any longer than necessary.

Novices and even experienced writers breaking into a prestigious market wield less clout than seasoned veterans, when it comes to negotiating their fees. Still, no writer ever lost an assignment with a legitimate magazine for bargaining politely and fairly. Realize that editors do have budgetary constraints and don't overstate your qualifications. If it's our first time writing for the magazine, we'll most likely be offered its regular rates. If we've already written two or three pieces requiring little editing or rewriting (unless it was for reasons beyond our control, such as a business we covered going bankrupt), then we should be asking for a raise. What you ask is determined by your writing experience and your negotiating skills. If you've written several pieces at forty cents a word, I think it's fair to ask for fifty. Mark and I do know of one long-time writer who begins every negotiation with an incredulous, "Is that all?" His style may not be for everyone.

Some magazines may ask you to write on speculation. You submit an article "on spec" and if it meets the editor's approval, the magazine may buy it. When I started writing I would work on spec for a magazine once, if it appeared to be a potential market for future work. After that, I expected a firm assignment. Now that I have experience it's unlikely I would ever work on speculation.

I have one final tip that worked for me when I first started writing. Some editors assign you a story quoting the total fee rather than a per-word rate. Off the top of my head I could never calculate whether $300 for a two-thousand-word story was a good deal. So I pinned up a little chart by my phone. Glancing at it, I immediately knew I was looking at a fifteen-cents-per-word assignment. I would then counter with $360, bringing my rate up to twenty cents a word.

Our Nickel or Theirs?

Find out, also, for which expenses the magazine will reimburse you. It's an industry standard that they pick up the tab for long-distance telephone calls, perhaps with a limit such as "not to exceed $100." I don't work for magazines that refuse to cover any long-distance calls at all.

Magazines should also pay a mileage fee if you have to drive outside your home town for interviews. I always try for forty-five cents a kilometre. This covers gas, maintenance, and your travelling time. Again, I have a chart by my phone that lets me know the mileage to and from various cities in my area. If an editor asks me to drive to Penticton, a 270-kilometre round trip, I ask for $120.

Unless I am writing a profile where I need a face-to-face interview or taking photographs, the magazine often finds it cheaper to have me conduct interviews by phone. I benefit financially, too. The time I save by not driving, I devote to writing.

If a magazine won't reimburse you for travelling expenses, try negotiating another assignment with a magazine that will and then conduct your interviews for both stories on the same trip.

If I'm taking photographs for the magazine I try to negotiate fifty dollars per photo. Often the magazine needs only one photo but I have to purchase and develop an entire roll of film (about twenty-five dollars for colour slides). Sometimes, though, magazines have a set fee, often as low as ten dollars; worse yet, they might insist the writing fee includes the cost of photos. In these cases, attempt to get the magazine to cover at least the cost of film and developing. (Be cautious of magazines that provide you with film. They often keep the photos for themselves, eliminating your chance to re-market them.)

Magazines sometimes cover other expenses such as research material, fax, and courier costs. Find out beforehand. If magazines send you far from home, as they often do with Mark, they pay for airfare, hotels, meals, and car rentals. It's reasonable to get an advance for at least the airfare and the accommodation. Otherwise you end up putting it on your charge card and waiting for your expense money to pay it off. If they don't offer an advance, ask for one.

The last money matter you should discuss is a kill fee. If, for some reason, a story is not published — perhaps a competitor just ran a similar story — some magazines pay a writer a percentage (up to 100 percent) of the negotiated fee. This kill fee compensates a writer for the time already committed to the story before it was "killed" and the writer is free to seek another home for the story. Kill fees are not standard and must be negotiated. Any writer consistently writing for the top markets should demand one.

You Want It When?

Deadline is the final point to cover with your editor. If you can't provide the story when it is needed, don't take on the assignment. If the unexpected happens, a house fire or car accident, let the editor know immediately and try for an extension. Writers who don't make deadline are unemployed writers.

Writers in the boonies (especially in the West and possibly the Maritimes) should allow ten days for their manuscripts to reach Toronto by mail. If the editor has a tight deadline, I ask if I can send the story collect by an overnight courier service. Of course, if the manuscript delay is my fault, I pay for the courier. Manuscripts to regional magazines can often be delivered, quickly and cheaply, by bus. Some magazines also accept manuscripts by fax or computer modem.

The Dotted Line

Now that we've negotiated the best possible assignment, it only remains to get it in writing. Using a contract like the Periodical Writers Association of Canada's Standard Freelance Publication Agreement (see the Appendix) ensures that both writer and magazine meet their obligations. Writers should fill in the contract (either PWAC's or one of their own choosing or design) with the negotiated details and submit two signed contracts to the editor, with instructions to sign and return one copy.

Occasionally, editors send out their own contract or assignment letter. These tend to favour the magazine, so read with care and, if necessary, negotiate changes. *Canadian*, the in-flight magazine for Canadian Airlines, had an exemplary assignment letter. Their editor confirmed the storyline with content suggestions and provided information on length, payment (upon invoice and acceptance), expense allowances, and deadline. (The magazine was recently sold and neither of us has yet had an opportunity to work for the new publishers.)

I must admit that I don't use a contract myself. If the magazine doesn't provide an assignment letter I send a letter of confirmation, a quick note covering the assignment specifics. I doubt this has any legal value, but it gives an editor a chance to let me know whether I've misunderstood; whether I really heard *fifteen* cents, not fifty.

I know I should use a contract, although I've yet to be stung, but time is always a problem for us boonie writers. If I lived in Toronto I could drop off the contract at the editor's office soon after I received the assignment. Living out here in the boonies, I must rely on Canada Post. If it takes five days for my contract to reach Toronto and another couple of days for the editor to pop it back in the mail, it could be two weeks or more before I had it in hand and could begin my assignment. However, by working without one, I'm taking the same risk as if I started an assignment while waiting for the contract to be mailed back to me. With hindsight, I would have got into the habit of using a contract right from the start of my career.

I always meet my deadlines, do my best to provide my editor with a good story, and negotiate the most equitable financial deal possible. And so should you. Just get it in writing.

CHAPTER FOUR

It's a Source, of Course

Research is a dirty word. At least it is to most magazine writers. The reason you get into this racket is you enjoy writing. But as we have seen in the previous three chapters, before the writing ever begins there is, and always will be, the need to research an idea sufficiently to develop a query. Upon assignment you conduct even more research. In simple terms, you need research material to write an article. The reality of magazine work is that writers spend far more time involved in research than in writing.

Researching an article usually takes at least three times as long as writing, rewriting, and putting the final polish on the piece. This leads you to think a magazine writer is less a writer than a professional researcher. Ah, but take heart. Anyone can research a subject and develop a weighty file of information. The special talent a magazine writer brings to research is the ability to take all that information, condense it, and then present it in an article that is as entertaining to read as it is informative.

So you had an idea, pitched it to an editor, and got an assignment. Where do you go now? Well, if the article is about a particular person, business, arts group, or the like, where you probably go is to the source — the chief executive officer of the company, or the executive director of the arts group — for an interview. The subject of interviews is so important to the magazine-writing process that I hoodwinked Louise into writing the next chapter on it, so we won't get into it too much here.

There are, however, many times when the article subject doesn't suggest an obvious source for an authoritative interview. If you are writing about trends in housing prices across the country, analysing what people can personally do to stave off the greenhouse effect, or detailing what to look for when buying a home computer, an immediate interview source might not spring to mind.

This is when most writers think of heading for the library, which is precisely where we now go.

Too Much, Too Little, Too Late

When I first became a boonie writer, I would enter my local library with a dark scowl on my face and look about gloomily at the meagre rows of books, the scarcity of magazines, the paltry stacks of newspapers, and the notable absence of resource staff to aid my research efforts. In a fit of despair I imagined big-city magazine writers whizzing efficiently about amid rows upon rows of books and fully stocked magazine sections, and calling upon the professional skill of dozens of eager resource people who would tap into data bases and offer up clipping files on a host of arcane topics. Generally, I saw myself as facing a woeful disadvantage because the libraries available to me simply could not compete.

Pushing aside my misgivings, I started digging through the microfiche indexes in search of appropriate books. I really don't remember what article I was working on when I first faced the library research crisis, so let's look at one I did recently on the ins and outs of buying and selling rental property as an investment. The article, for a major business magazine, required a thorough handling of not only what an investor should do but also what the current rental property market was like across the country.

Sorting through the subject indexes I found a number of books that seemed relevant to the subject of rental property investment. From the shelves I pulled five books containing around half a million words on the subject I was to cover in thirty-five hundred. Words, words, and more words swam before my eyes. How could I possibly assimilate all this and condense it into a magazine article? This was beyond even the compression skills of *Reader's Digest.*

Gamely I started reading my way through the first book and within pages knew something was wrong with my research method. The first book talked about how an investor could realize a healthy profit with a rental rate of $150 per month for a side-by-side duplex. The second book advised investors to shun residential rental property in city cores because of the movement of the middle classes to the suburbs.

Here I was with half a million words — half a million old, no longer true, words. Checking the copyright dates listed inside, I found only one of the books had been published in the past year. Even this book no longer covered the current market conditions.

I realized again something I forget when I try to research an article from books in the library. Magazines deal in now. Outside of historical magazines there is little interest in how things worked twenty years ago, a year ago, or even a few months ago. A magazine editor wants an article that deals with what is happening this minute.

Each time this realization strikes me, I look about the library and smile. I gloat. It all comes home to me in these moments. Libraries are full of information; they are full of old, outdated information. Those shelves hold little of use to the magazine writer.

This is as true for magazine writers in metropolitan centres as it is for those living in the boonies. In this case I dropped the half million dated words on a rack for reshelving, packed up my notebook, and walked directly to the reference section.

Guides to Sources

In the reference section of any library, big or small, a writer finds what is needed to research any article. In those books that cannot be taken out of the library we find sources. And sources are the be-all and end-all of magazine research.

A source is a person who can fill you in on aspects of your subject in terms of what is happening *now.* They are experts. They are university professors. Presidents of professional associations. Statisticians working for the government. All are credible sources with access to current information. And they're easy to find.

In the library reference section are a host of information almanacs. These are publications that list addresses, phone numbers, and contact names of associations, societies, businesses, government agencies, and almost any other body that might have specialized knowledge or information. Almanacs have titles like *Information Please*, *Canadian Almanac & Directory*, or *Sources*. For a magazine writer they are utterly wonderful. In minutes, they provide research leads to almost any topic.

Take the rental-property investment piece. From the almanacs I gleaned contact names and phone numbers at a national real-estate agency. This agency has a statistics department which tracks the financial ups and downs of the market city by city, as well as provincially and nationally. The information is calculated every four months and that is as close to now as you can get on this subject.

The almanacs also provided contacts in government agencies monitoring rental-property sales and investment figures, sources at city real-estate boards across the country, several tenant associations, and the names of a host of financial analysts at major investment companies and accounting firms who could offer their expert opinions on how to play the investment game.

After jotting down this information I turned to one last untapped library asset — the periodical indexes Louise mentioned in Chapter Two. Undoubtedly your article subject has been touched on by other writers. So it makes sense to check the subject listings of the indexes and take note of these articles. Then, and this might be hard if your local library is like some in the boonies and carries few magazines, try to find the magazine articles for the names of experts and other sources who have been tapped for their knowledge on your subject.

Note their names and where they work and live. There is nothing plagiaristic about doing this. It is only plagiarism if you steal their previously published quotes and incorporate them into your article. If, however, you take the names of the people and contact them yourself, you will be getting new information. Anyone who isn't an automaton phrases what he says differently each time he deals with a subject. What you get from this source bears little resemblance to what was carried in other articles.

The advantage of checking other articles for prospective sources is a simple one. Some of the sources you draw from almanacs have no interest in talking to you, are impossible to reach, or are prohibited by company policy or some other rule from discussing the matter with you. Sources, however, who have already talked about the subject with one writer will likely talk about it with another. Using these obviously willing sources shortens the research process, eliminating the time spent contacting prospective sources who decline to give you information.

There is one cautionary note that should be made when consulting other magazines. You may find that the quote you get from the source is not as enlightening or entertaining as that given earlier to another magazine writer. This may lead you to think it would be a good idea simply to quote the source from the other magazine and credit that publication in your article. You know, something like: "In *Maclean's*, John What's-His-Name said . . . " No plagiarism here because the source is credited and it's all above board, right?

True, but it is taboo to quote another magazine in most magazine articles, since virtually all magazines can be considered to be in competition. Come to that, you notice there are no quotes in this book from other magazine-article writing guides. That would not fly either.

There is one isolated condition where citing other magazines in an article is appropriate. This is when you counterpoint attitudes towards a subject. Take an avant-garde artist, for example. You want to counterpoint critical reaction to her work. In this case it would be effective to write: "Leda Glitz's ironic sculptures of ostriches striking manly poses have been hailed by the art critic of *The New Yorker* as visionary and panned as commercialized trash by Wilma Meyer of the authoritative *Avant-Garde Art Today Magazine*." Quoting two respected magazines dealing with the arts immediately rams home that Glitz is to be taken seriously even if the art world can't agree on the value of her work.

In most cases, however, the best rule of thumb is to avoid mentioning the names of other magazines in your articles and even shun references to books, unless the information is vital to the article.

Have Sources, Will Research

Having gathered a fat list of possible sources, you return to your office and start working the telephone. These calls should be billable to the magazine commissioning the article. If not, use sources close to home or make tactical use of time differences to get long-distance discounts. Sometimes your sources won't be available when you call. Leave your name and the nature of the article you are writing with a request that they call you collect. Most call back on their own dime and often within the day.

These usually brief calls to information sources are not so much interviews as information-gathering sessions. Other than the name, position, and organization to which the source is linked you do not learn much about the person you contact. You are not talking to these people to find out how many children they have, what their hobbies are, or how much they earn annually. They hold information on the subject you are researching. Confine your questions as much as possible to that. Many of these people are going to be extremely busy and you may only have a few minutes of their time. Don't waste it. Get as much information as you can and if they say they have to go, don't harass them into staying on the phone. Rather, find out when they might be free again and phone back. When you have what you need, end the call and move on to the next source on your list.

Avoid duplication of information. If you have talked to two similar sources and they cover the same points, forget about phoning another source who falls into the same category. All you are likely to get is the same material over again. Look instead to your source list for someone who might offer a different opinion.

Remember the rental-property investment piece? If all the realtors you talk to extol the virtues of buying a rental property and then selling it quickly when the market is hot, maybe it's time to phone a few representatives of tenant associations to see who they feel is benefitting. Landlords or tenants?

Look for conflicting opinions and consider yourself lucky if two experts disagree. Including both views in the article shows balance and objectivity on your part. Magazine editors prefer this to espousals of one belief at the expense of another. Try to strike a balance in the sources you contact and quote in your article.

After a number of calls — it may be three or thirty depending on your subject — you notice you are hearing the same thing repeated over and over. This usually indicates there is little to be found in further research. It's time to quit.

When I finish my research, the first thing I do is transcribe my scrawled notes into type. It may be a few days before I get back to this information and there is nothing more devastating than illegible notes. Remember what I said about these people being busy? Imagine what they will think if I have to phone them again to decipher my scribbling.

Cherish Your Sources

The main reason for treating your sources with respect and courtesy is that a good contact is like money in the bank. Over the years, I have acquired a hefty listing of experts who are not only knowledgeable but talented at providing the perfectly worded anecdote to highlight a point. These sources are invaluable and I go out of my way to curry their favour.

I ensure they get copies of the articles in which they have been quoted even if the magazine is uncooperative and I have to buy them off the newsstand or send them photocopies. When I call them again, I always remind them of who I am and what article I last quoted them in.

Sources have varying reasons for talking to writers. For some, it's their job to talk to you or anyone else who calls. For others, it is good promotion for themselves, their business, or their society to be quoted as expert sources in a magazine article. Sometimes personal vanity enters into it — they just like seeing themselves in print. When you go back to a source a couple of times, you probably come to understand the reason that person talks to you. If a reliable source is vain, why not drop his name? Don't overplay this hand but do quote him when he's relevant and credit him for the information. Even the sources who are required by their job to talk to you are likely to be pleased to see their names in print. In your article, name the government statisticians you interviewed. Unless the sources have told you something out of school or off the record (in which case you will likely want to protect them with anonymity), it lends more legitimacy to your article if "Jane Doe of Statistics Canada says," rather than, "A source in Statistics Canada says."

Even a valuable source should never be allowed to abuse you. If a previously excellent source tries to make you write something you know is not factual or to put an unfair slant on a subject, refuse to do it. This often happens with good business sources. A stockbroker who had been a terrific conduit to people in the know on a host of financial matters once tried to get me to hype a company he was promoting. He urged me to mention the company in my article. When I declined because it was of little relevance, he got snitty and I lost him as a source.

Losing him was a small blow, not a disaster. The thing about sources is that there are always more just a phone call away, and if you treat them fairly, they will probably be there the next time you need them. Good thing, because without their expertise, we would have little to back up our magazine articles.

CHAPTER
FIVE

Don't Tell Anybody, But . . .

I didn't suspect a thing when the old guy relieved me of my notepad and pen and handed me the reins. Suddenly I was scrambling up the mountainside behind the back end of a very large Belgian-cross that knew a lot more about horse logging than I did. Half an hour later, I had discovered how much these draft animals cost, what they ate, and the best way to master horse logging (let the horse teach you). I would learn more. Not as much as the horse already knew, mind you, but more than enough to satisfy a magazine editor or reader.

Not all interviews take place in a soft early-morning mist on the side of a timber-rich mountain. Sometimes they happen in a crowded restaurant or a stuffy office. But no matter where you conduct them, interviews provide the quotes, anecdotes, and galvanizing facts that empower your writing.

For me, they're at once the best part of magazine writing and the most frustrating. Interviews are fun. I've sampled award-winning cuisine, polled financiers about their underwear preferences, and witched (unsuccessfully) for water with a forked branch. I've chatted with artists, athletes, and agricultural gamblers. I've discovered that ginseng farming is addictive and llamas are beguiling pets. Still, even with the most informative and revealing interview, there's always the niggling sense that I could have elicited sharper quotes, stronger narratives, or deeper insights.

I'm beginning to realize, however, that interviewing is like making love. The more you do it, the better you get. Use the following guidelines to get started. Then it's only a matter of developing skills and your own style. Fortunately, as with sex, the practice sessions are enjoyable, too.

Be Prepared

Start your interview before you ever leave home. Dig up some basic facts. Read articles on similar topics. Make a list of questions. Like the Boy Scouts, be prepared.

Not many stories from the boonies are about famous people, huge corporations, or earth-rattling events, so there may not be much background material available. If you interview a local ginseng farmer, you're not likely to find him in any *Who's Who*, but you will find information on ginseng. Skim through it and get an idea what ginseng farming is like: its history and markets, the equipment costs, the risks. Note the details other articles provide. This gives you an idea what your editor (and your readers) expect.

Now you can begin a list of questions. I jot them down on scrap paper in random order and organize them later. Looking back at my notes, I see I looked up ginseng in several herbal guides and a gardening book. Here are some questions that came to mind. Number of acres under cultivation? Climate requirements? Potential harvest per acre? Current price of ginseng? Start-up costs?

I also learned that ginseng is very finicky and yields a marketable harvest only every four years. I added these questions to my list: How risky is ginseng farming? What's the most worthwhile aspect of this venture?

Avoid listing questions that can be answered with a simple yes or no. You want your subjects to respond with emotion, recall events in living colour, make predictions. A good all-purpose question is, Why is that? This encourages people to expand on their experiences and opinions, giving you meaty prose to pass on to your readers.

This is also a good way to get background information on a complex topic. Something like this: "For readers who don't have a financial background, can you explain the advantages of option trades?"

Once I have a lengthy list of questions, I group them into an order that's, to me at least, logical and consistent. Even though I won't necessarily ask the questions in that sequence, I set up my question sheet the same way for every interview.

I write "name" at the top. This reminds me to get the correct spelling of my subject's name, degrees, job title, and company. Business cards are great for this and I always ask for one. Verify the information on the card. I also get a mailing address for an eventual thank-you note. Often you can get this material beforehand, perhaps from a receptionist or the yellow pages of the telephone book. Then I continue with age, education, and background. Now I'm up to the crucial questions, the ones I need answered before I leave the interview. In the ginseng story I listed all the money questions. How much is seed? Equipment? First year's profit or loss? At the end I jot a note to ask about future plans and for names of other contacts.

Remember, you won't necessarily ask the questions in this order. If your subjects are nervous, asking about the mundane things first, like education background, can help relax them. More assertive people, on the other hand, might prefer you to jump right in with the challenging questions. Why did you choose this profession? Why is your company succeeding when others are going under?

Some interviews go so smoothly you find you hardly refer to your list. At other times it can be a lifesaver: providing a question when your brain has turned to mush and your mouth to cotton, keeping you on topic, and ensuring that you leave the interview with the critical answers.

Pencil or Tape Recorder?

The interview session during my workshop is terrific fun. Participants get a chance to interview each other, often discovering talented, fascinating people — and potential magazine stories — right in their own community. After deciphering their hastily written notes, they always ask the same question: Do you use a tape recorder for your interviews? And I answer, "Only if I have to."

Tape recorders are great. You don't have to worry about missing a dynamic quote. Instead of scribbling away madly you can make eye contact with your subject. And you have an accurate record of your interview.

They appear to have few drawbacks. You may interview someone who is intimidated by a tape recorder, although such people are becoming rarer in this era of electronic gadgets. You could have equipment failure, a not-so-rare occurrence. Fresh batteries and a periodic check of your recording prevents that disaster. So why don't I always use a tape recorder? You have to transcribe the tapes. It's perhaps the only disadvantage but to me it's a colossal aggravation. I can't think of anything more boring than playing and replaying a tape until I manage to type out all the pertinent facts and quotes.

In simple interviews, I'm able to keep up with my version of speed writing. I use my question list to jot facts like number of acres, start-up costs, and the like into the appropriate blanks. With the questions always arranged in a similar order, it's easy to slot in these numerical statistics while keeping my notepad handy for quotes and anecdotes.

Here's where I rely on my tape recorder (plus a few hand-written notes in case the machine fails): *always* for a major interview. Say, the chief executive officer of western Canada's largest tire dealer. Or actor Kevin Costner. The tire executive was only in town for the day. If I missed something in my notes I wouldn't be able to phone for immediate clarification. The same with Kevin Costner. If he came to my hometown and I was able to secure an interview, it would most likely be a one-shot deal.

I'd tape an interview with **Gonzo** journalism creator Hunter S. Thompson. Or the protagonists in a Chamber of Commerce dispute. It's a good idea to record any interview on a contentious topic or with a querulous subject. Then tuck the tapes away against the unlikely chance that you might have to substantiate your story in court.

I also find taping handy when I'm interviewing two people at once. The Smothers Brothers. Or the founding partners of an expanding fabric store. Two people tend to build on each other's energy, jogging sluggish memories, one-upping anecdotes. Your pencil may not keep up. As long as you can tell Tommy's voice from Dick's, your tape recorder will safeguard their sibling banter.

Tape recorders do have one other advantage over handwritten notes. They let you listen to your interview. Every so often, record an interview and then assess your skills. Are you jumping in to fill up every moment of silence? Are you cutting off your subjects just when they're ready to open up? Are you doing all the talking? If you answer yes to any of the above, don't pass go, don't collect two hundred dollars, and don't skip the next section.

Tactics

Silence can be golden — in the countryside, on an early-morning walk, after the kids go to bed. But it's darn awkward in a conversation, especially with people we don't know. We tend to smooth over the lulls with small talk. Remember, though, interviews are not conversation. We may start off chatting, putting our subjects at ease by sharing a bit of ourselves, but we're really there to listen. We want to hear our subjects' experiences. Their opinions. Their emotions.

Value the silent intervals. Give people time to collect their thoughts and they may reward you with the perfect quote or example. On the other hand, if the silence unnerves them, they may jump in with a spicy bit of news or a revealing anecdote. Either way, you win.

While your subjects ruminate on their replies, use the time to check out their surroundings. Our mothers told us it's impolite to be nosy, but they didn't have interviews in mind. Profiles, especially, call for lots of revealing details. Where is the interview taking place? If it's an office, note its size, furnishings, and, if possible, compare its location and amenities to other offices in the company. Is it bland and utilitarian or are there lots of mementos and knick-knacks? Does your subject smoke? What brand? Bite his nails? Wear scuffed Boulet cowboy boots? Pristine Nikes? Look for clues to your subject's personality.

You're lucky if you get to interview people in their homes. Then you can note their decorating tastes, what they read, the music they listen to, their hobbies. These details can tell us as much as, or more than, our subjects' actual words.

Allow the interview to meander, occasionally. As people relax they tend to drift off topic. These unplanned forays are often the most rewarding part of the interview. If you let your subject digress, you may learn that the president of the ginseng association plays golf and attended the Banff School of Fine Arts. If your story is strictly about ginseng, you probably won't use this information. But if the president happens to go on and mention the sexual benefits of a certain ginseng regime, you suddenly have a dynamite anecdote to highlight the root's medicinal properties. These leisurely interviews aren't always necessary or practical, but if I have the time (and the patience), I let my subjects set the interview's pace and direction.

Don't confuse the combative interviews on television with the interviews we conduct for a print story. Our job as magazine writers is to gather information and then present it in a form that's entertaining. Unlike television or radio, where the interviewer is in the spotlight almost as much as the subject, magazines show only the results of our interview. The interview itself is not a media event. We're not performers; we don't have to worry about show biz or ratings. Our aim is to create a relaxed atmosphere where people feel free to tell their stories. For us, good manners go a long way to ensuring a good interview.

I'm going to interrupt Louise for a moment to comment on one time in magazine interviewing when poor manners are advantageous. Lengthy face-to-face interviews are seldom conducted in a vacuum. During the time you are together your subject will likely be interrupted by people and events unrelated to the interview. Standard rules of politeness suggest you turn off your ears during this time and wait patiently until the interview can resume. This is fine if you're doing an article on how an industrial psychologist diagnoses burnout on the job and the psychologist's spouse has called to discuss where they might eat that night. But if you're talking to a land developer who is assembling a deal on the phone, don't be shy — eavesdrop. This may be the ultimate chance to see this person in action, providing a wonderful illustration of the reality of a land developer's life.

These moments when your interview subject is pursuing the normal round right before your eyes are the best opportunities to gather the dramatic material you want for the article's introduction and conclusion. I talk more about this in the next chapter, but for now, keep in mind the interview is more than the dialogue between the two of you.

Particularly when doing personality or lifestyle profiles, you are looking for occasions where your subjects reveal their inner selves. For this same reason it is useful to get them mobile. If you interview a legendary country musician who also is a working cowboy, then do as much of your interview as possible while he is out shoeing horses or rounding up cattle. If it's an interview with a world-class chef, why not talk in the kitchen as culinary wonders are being prepared? The worst that can happen is that you get saddle-sores, or tomato sauce splotches on your notepad. But you might also witness the sloppiest chef in the land or a cowboy singer who lassoes a calf with a Houlihan throw as skilfully as the most seasoned cowpuncher. Both provide drama and colour for your article.

Finally, never dismiss the seemingly trivial incidents that occur during an interview. If your subject stops the interview to have a short dialogue with a son or daughter, listen to the words exchanged and write them down. People often divulge themselves in these moments more than they ever will in the formal interview itself. The way your subject relates to the child might prove a fascinating ingredient for your article.

So be polite, but never be afraid to spy. In Chapter Ten I look at how far this covert surveillance should go. But for now, back to Louise.

Tact

Dress to put your subject at ease. For an interview with an oil executive at his corporate office, I'd probably wear a suit. If the interview was taking place at the drilling field, I'd wear jeans and boots. No one would have confidence in my ability to write about the company if I showed up at the rig site in heels and a skirt. And if I wore shorts and thongs to the office, I wouldn't project the image of someone able to discuss the financial aspects of a resource industry.

We can wear what we like while conducting telephone interviews. Even bunny slippers. I used to do all my interviews in person if I could. Now, to cut down on travelling time, I do many over the phone. A short phone interview is very effective when you're after specific information. People don't tend to ramble as much and yet they're often more candid. This is also the only practical way to interview people across the country.

Set up your interview at a time that's convenient for your subjects. You have better interviews when they're not distracted by ringing phones, customers, or crying babies. This applies to phone interviews, too. When you call, ask if it's a convenient time to talk.

At first, I was uncomfortable requesting interviews. It was easier if I already had a firm assignment. Then I could say, "*The Financial Post Magazine* has asked me to write a story on your boxer shorts. Is there a good time for us to get together?" If I was still in the hunting stage I tried, "I'm proposing a story on post-partum depression to *Chatelaine* and I'd like to talk to you about your clinic."

I quickly discovered that people are thrilled to talk about themselves or an area of their expertise. I haven't had anyone turn me down yet. As Mark pointed out in the previous chapter, it's beneficial to many business people and professionals to have their names in print, to be quoted as an expert in their field. They're willing, even eager, to answer your questions. While you appreciate the time they've taken to talk to you, don't feel they're doing you a favour. It's an equal opportunity. You get the information, they get the publicity. On the other hand, they don't owe you an interview. If they don't want to talk to you, that's their prerogative.

Never pay for an interview. Don't be browbeaten into including information you wouldn't normally use in return for the material you've been given. And be prepared to say no when your subject asks to read the article before it goes to the magazine. Blame it on the magazine. Say, "Sorry, my editor insists on being the first to read my stuff."

Occasionally, I do allow people to check select portions of a manuscript, for example, to ensure that my statement of a physician's medical evaluation of the symptoms of advanced diabetes is correct. But if the story were a profile, I would not let the physician read my work and perhaps take umbrage at my observations of hand gestures and such. Readers count on us to bring integrity to our articles. Sometimes this puts us and our subjects at odds. But we can't allow ourselves to be coerced into changing a story simply to satisfy our subjects' vanity. (Larger magazines do employ fact checkers to double-check facts and quotes in your story before it goes to print. More about that in Chapter Seven.)

Sometimes you have awkward or difficult questions to ask. Work up to them gradually. And then phrase them as tact-fully as possible. Something like this: "Some people believe your attitude towards women is insensitive and archaic. What do you say to them?" Another good ploy is to blame it on the boss. "I'm uncomfortable doing this, but my editor insists I ask your age." Of course, if you feel the best approach is to be blunt, give "Why are you so hostile to immigrants?" a try.

It surprises me how willing people are to discuss a thorny issue. In my naïvete, I used to think my superb interviewing was lulling them into a false security and compelling them to confide in me. I realize now they said nothing they didn't want me to hear. Occasionally, they may have exercised poor judgement and blurted something they later regretted, but from the start, they were aware I was a writer and recording everything they said.

Can I Use This?

You must identify yourself as a writer. Don't eavesdrop on environmental activist and scientist David Suzuki at a private party and then quote him in your story. You could identify yourself as a writer and then question him, although he might resent the intrusion into his private time. You'd be more likely to get a productive interview if you asked, instead, whether you could arrange to talk at another time. If, however, Suzuki is addressing a public function, feel free to quote him. And you might have a chance to grill him during a question period or on his way out. In this case Suzuki has assumed his public persona, so trying to get a quote from him is fair play.

You can use everything your subjects tell you unless they say it's "off the record." Often these off-the-record remarks give you valuable background information, help you understand a controversial issue, or provide leads to other sources. Your subject must tell you it's off the record first. It's too late if he reveals a fabulous story and then says, "By the way, you can't use any of this." Whether you use it or not depends on the situation and your sense of ethics. (Mark expands on this in Chapter Ten.)

Sometimes a subject tells you something that's "not for attribution." This means you can use the information, but you can't say who told you. Newspapers often quote "a senior federal-government spokesman" or "an industry representative." This isn't as common in magazines. With their longer lead time, magazine editors usually expect you to drum up an identifiable source.

Closing Shop

If your subjects set aside an hour for you, respect their time restriction. Pace yourself. Cover the important questions before the hour is up. If subjects are willing to extend an interview and you feel it's worth your time, take advantage of their generosity. Before you conclude the interview, scan your notes for missed questions. Give people the opportunity to add anything they feel is important that you may have missed asking about. Ask whether you can call back if you have further questions and whether they'll be unavailable because of upcoming events or trips. Thank them for their time, pack up your stuff, and say goodbye. But stay alert. For some reason — perhaps because they're more relaxed or just had time to think — people often tell you the best story just as you're leaving. On my way out the door I once learned what one woman really thought of her bankers. If your mind is on picking up a pizza on the way home, think what you could miss.

Tidying Up

Few people speak concisely during an interview for a magazine article. Your subject says, "Where I, uh, grew up on the Prairies, there were a lot of, uh, fields of, you know, that grain they make the oil out of, the one with the funny name, uh, canola I think it's called." You could write, "There were a lot of canola fields on the Prairies where I grew up."

There are purists in the journalistic community who say even this benign tinkering with a subject's words constitutes unacceptable distortion. However, editors, and the subjects themselves, expect their thoughts and opinions to be presented clearly, not lost in the stop-and-go, unfinished sentences most of us use in conversation. No one will be upset if you take out the "ums" and "ahs" and forge their words into a strong, cohesive sentence, but they will be upset if you use their words out of context.

"I'm against farmers using pesticides unless there's no other viable defence," says your subject. It would be wrong for you to lop this quote down to, "I'm against farmers." That's not what your subject was saying. It is acceptable to tidy up quotes for brevity or clarity, but you must adhere scrupulously to your subject's intended meaning.

Most people ramble and digress, only to return to a former topic, adding further details throughout the interview. To make a coherent story, you can piece together information from various portions of the interview or interviews (sometimes you have the chance to talk on more than one occasion). Here's an example: "There were a lot of canola fields on the Prairies where I grew up. Of course, it was called rapeseed in those days and simply cultivated as a forage crop for the livestock. Cholesterol wasn't a hot topic yet." These sentences were spoken at different times during the interview, but each referred to the subject's perception of the history of canola. Again, the rule is to respect the subject's words and not rearrange them to present a false meaning.

New writers are often tempted to sanitize a subject's colourful language. This is one area where you should avoid editing. In cleaning up their words, we can scour the colour right out of the quote. Some people use words like "ain't" to great advantage. To correct their grammar would rob the quote of any authenticity. Excising a corny "by cracky" or an expletive can have the same effect. If your subject says "shit" and it's a telling detail, leave it in.

Include the juicy anecdotes, emotional confessions, and daring pronouncements if they, too, add to your story. Don't use them, though, if they're just sensational padding. This can be tough, knowing when to quote a subject and when to use your own words, knowing what to keep and what to discard. Experience helps. So does Mark's advice in the next chapter.

CHAPTER SIX

Writing Well

The day has finally arrived. Earlier you wrote a snappy query, wooed an editor, pinned an assignment, finagled the best pay you could, made like Dick Tracy doing the research. Now you are ready to do what first prompted you to enter the magazine field — *write.*

You gather your notes. The blank computer screen or the page in the typewriter waits. All that is missing is those first impressive sentences to make the editor laugh, cry, and desperately want an encore. The clock ticks. The words just are not there. Are you about to be revealed as a dismal amateur?

All writers have this ingrained doubt every time they start a new writing project. What if the magic is gone? What if it never really existed? We are our own worst enemies. It's the fear we will not be able to write, or at least not well, that holds us back and hurts our careers.

In magazine writing, the problem is sometimes more acute than in other writing pursuits because we sense it is impossible to write a non-fiction article creatively. How do we tackle the subject within editorial requirements in a style that will make for entertaining reading?

We cast about for inspiration. The pile of research notes sits lumpily by our right elbow, trying to catch our eye. We need a guide to take us from beginning to end, covering all salient points. We remember high school and university. We remember that old helpmate, the outline. This is it, we gloat, this is the key. It will be like playing with building blocks.

Just plop the outline's individual blocks one on top of the other and voilà — we have an article.

And we do, too: a clunky, blocked-together article evoking only a bored yawn from our editor.

Flick Your Bic

When I started writing for a living in the 1970s, I worked in the pressure-cooker environment of a newspaper. There was no time here to write outlines. Stories were written in minutes, rather than hours. You learned to write on demand. In later years I was introduced to a technique for spontaneous writing called freefall, which provided a perspective on what I had been doing to meet newspaper deadlines.

Freefall has been used for years by fiction writers. The term was supposedly first coined by W.O. Mitchell, Prairie novelist and for many years an instructor at the Banff School of Fine Arts summer creative-writing program. Freefall shuns outlines. Show freefallers an outline and the first thing they'll do is put a Bic lighter to it.

The reasoning is simple. How can you possibly draft an outline when you don't yet know the story? And if you know the story, why do you need an outline?

Magazine writing is a creative process — a quest for the most evocative way to relate a story. This initial search is better pursued in a first draft than by a painfully constructed outline.

First drafts are not finished work. Forget word-count requirements, sentence and paragraph transitions, grammatic exactitude. Seek instead to blend images, statistics, quotes, and other ingredients unearthed in your research in the way that most vividly tells the tale.

Before writing anything, read over your research notes. Repeatedly. This imprints the information in your memory so you won't often have to look up specific details in your notes to confirm what someone said, what something looked like, what a statistic revealed. You won't remember quotes exactly and might be off a little in some statistics, but these can be corrected later. The trick now is just to feel that you know this information as well as someone cramming for a university exam.

Now begin the first draft. Where? It doesn't matter, really. The idea is to start writing and keep writing until you feel that everything you need to tell the story has been transferred from mind to paper.

To kickstart yourself, ask questions like these. What is the most significant fact in this story? Historically, when did this story begin? Which character is most important? Is one physical image stronger than the others? Depending on the nature of the story, the answer to one of these questions will seem most relevant. Start there.

Take your time writing. Thoroughly depict each aspect of the story. Don't worry about writing too much. Right now there is no such thing as excess. As you run out of things to say about the first story detail, think of the next most relevant piece of information, or where the completion of the first detail logically leads. Pick up that thread next. One point might require only a few words to cover, another several hundred. Continue this process until you exhaust all the material contained in your research.

You now have a completed first draft. Probably ragged looking and way over the assigned word count. However, start polishing those words, factual descriptions, and images and you discover the essential elements of an effective story. You also find an organic integrity that cinches the article together with a natural logic no outline could provide.

Rearrange the material so it flows smoothly from one detail to the next. Cut repetitions. Select from your descriptive passages the freshest prose, toss out the lifeless or clichéd images. Paraphrase long quotes to prevent a source from becoming a tedious lecturer. Retain quotes containing well-turned phrases, examples, images. Retool dull quotes by again paraphrasing what the source said, this time couching the idea in more dynamic language. Correct all errors in grammar, punctuation, and structure that crept in during the freefall writing phase. Think about what, if anything, you've left out that the editor wanted covered. Filter that material in. Ensure that quotes are exact and, if you have reworked the language, that the essence of what the source said has been retained. Check your research for any essential details you might have missed and work them in, if needed.

When this second draft is complete, it should read smoothly, feeling so natural you can't imagine a more effective telling. By now the article is close to the assigned length. If you are over, whittle things down to fit. Focus on descriptive passages and repetitive quotes. Usually this is where excess verbiage shows up.

Seldom does freefall yield too short an article. But if it does, mine your notes for missed anecdotes, statistics, and illuminating quotes. Avoid mere padding. You should render the article more vivid and informative, not merely clutter the page with words. If the new words add nothing and your notes reveal little of use, then these are good hints that your initial research was anaemic. Do some more.

As they gain experience with the method, most freefallers discover their first drafts require less reworking and often finish close to the required word length. At this stage, they have become controlled freefallers. Like veteran skydivers they can turn and angle with dexterity to control the plane of their descent, allowing themselves to plunge through an image quickly or, if need be, to hover in seeming defiance of the natural downward pull. In this phase, they may even weave about within the article, cutting and adding material, moulding it so the completed first draft is almost a finished piece of writing. How soon you reach this stage, or whether you ever do, is of little import. Your ability to freefall effectively evolves as you practise and develop your skill. The initial requirement is the most essential — trust yourself enough to take that first step into open space.

The Frugal Writer

I have to butt in here to reassure all those writers who are as tight with their words as I am. I heartily endorse Mark's enthusiasm for freefall. I just can't do it.

I edit as I write. I basically smooth out each paragraph before proceeding to the next. By the time I reach my conclusion the article requires only a final polish. However, this is false economy on my part.

As I delete and rearrange my words at my computer, I'm probably writing as much as Mark does in his unrestrained first drafts. I write, perfecting as I go, unaware of the trail of discarded words I've blipped away. But as long as I'm not confronted with them on my computer screen, I remain blissfully ignorant of how much I've actually written.

I do freefall as much as my frugal nature allows. While I can't write a paragraph without editing it before I proceed to the next, I do use the freefall technique of allowing the story to grow and shape itself as I write. Once I've nailed down the opening paragraph, which often accounts for a good half of my writing time, I'm home free. I like to link my conclusion to my lead, or opening hook, so that with a good idea of where the story is going, the remaining writing is relatively easy.

It seems I have to know my destination before I start to write, while Mark, the quintessential freefaller, discovers his direction as he writes.

Grabbing Your Reader by the Throat,
or
How to Write Scintillating Introductions

Whether you use pure freefall or Louise's more frugal approach, the elements that make your writing more dramatic and readable remain the same. In the final draft, first impressions are absolutely critical. The first words of an article must shine like dawn light reflecting off desert rock. Otherwise, you run the risk of losing your editor's attention.

Think about it for a minute and you will see how we all subject introductions to a severe test. Do you finish a book with a bland start? Do you flip past magazine articles with a dull opening?

In a world full of material crying out for our attention, we are becoming increasingly selective in what we read. Yet once we are hooked with a sparkling lead, we usually read the piece through to conclusion. We are all susceptible to the old foot-in-the-door routine. In writing terms, this means a good introduction that opens your mind just a crack and keeps the mental door from slamming when the pace begins to slow. Before you know it, you've bought the goods and read the entire article.

Let's look at the components of a successful introduction. The most obvious is a scene of high drama that draws the reader into the story. In Chapter One, I mentioned the *Reader's Digest* piece on the boy who was mauled by a dog. The attack was graphically rendered in the first few paragraphs. The writer went on to quote various experts' advice for preventing similar tragedies. The real point of the article was not to recount the mauling, but to relate the experts' recommendations. The account of the attack was simply a hook: a dramatic, strong, in this case violent incident that immediately engaged the reader's interest.

This technique is used to some degree in virtually every how-to magazine article, and that's a clear indication of how well it works. Whether it's how to diagnose bulimia in teenage girls, how to prevent a hostile corporate takeover, or how to firm up by lifting weights, there is no better start than to provide a brief personal story proving the point or asking the question, "What is to be done?"

In my business and personal-finance writing, I habitually use this technique. I continue my research, sometimes long after I have the expert opinions, until I secure the telling anecdote. Without it, I have little story.

Once, I wrote on the ins and outs of investing in penny stocks traded on the Vancouver Stock Exchange. These are stocks for dreamers — the same dreamers who buy lottery tickets. They hope to sell these cheap stocks for a killing when they suddenly rocket upward in value. It seldom happens, of course, but there are always more who are ready to plunk down their money and take the gamble.

For this article, there was no shortage of horror stories of gamblers who lost thousands and even millions on the pennies.

It took a long time, however, to come up with someone who was an eternal winner; when I did I had my introduction. This is how "Penny Whys: Playing with the VSE juniors is a risky but frisky game" began:

> Izzie Rotterman is a gambler who wins. For 40 years, the multimillionaire Torontonian has made millions investing in the high-risk junior securities listed on the Vancouver Stock Exchange (VSE), which often trade for several dollars a share, yet are commonly known as "penny stocks." "People say you can't make money investing on the Vancouver Stock Exchange. Well, I'm the proof that's not true," Rotterman says in his gravelly voice. Sure, he affirms, most people lose money buying penny stock. It's not because the investment is bad, he believes; it's because they don't have the gambler's courage and instinct that enable Rotterman and others to sense a bonanza stock and play it for all it's worth.

From there I went on to tell how Rotterman once rode a penny for $20 million. After allowing Izzie to sing his own praises, I slipped back from the dizzying heights of his success to ground zero, filling in the reader on what a penny stock was and adding sobering advice from other analysts who felt Izzie's was a hard act to follow.

Without Izzie's experience at the top, however, the article would have been a downer about broken dreams pursued by gamblers. Wouldn't we more likely read an article that offered some hope? In this case, the hope that we, too, might play the odds as well as Izzie?

The pennystock introduction is also an example of capturing reader attention with a good opening sentence. "Izzie Rotterman is a gambler who wins." Crisp, clean, and a fascinating contradiction. When an opportunity like this comes along, grab it.

That opening line freefell through my keyboard onto the screen the morning I began writing the article. It wasn't surprising. I knew I was going to begin with Izzie, and allowing my mind to do its thing, it opted for the direct route. That bald statement said far more than any long winded anecdote about his investing in one particular stock. It also ensured that I stayed within my rather short word count.

Sometimes you can't sum up your subject so precisely. It's just too broad. Your best introduction may be to have your characters in motion, grappling with the problem at hand. Again, this means fishing for the visual details to create a scene for the reader.

I used this technique when I wrote about Norman Keevil Sr., the late president and chairman of western Canada's maverick mining company, Teck Corporation. Keevil built his empire from scratch over a thirty-two-year career, but at the time I was writing the piece, he had just crowned its growth with a stunning takeover of one of Canada's largest and oldest mining corporations.

Normally, I would start a profile of an individual like Keevil with an anecdote from the early history of his career. Instead, I began with the final day of takeover.

> On October 16, four men gathered in a 14th-floor executive office overlooking Vancouver harbour and quietly celebrated the $280-million purchase of a 31-percent-controlling interest in a corporation holding $2 billion in assets. As Norman Keevil Sr. poured glasses of Dom Pérignon, his son, Norm Keevil Jr., and the "wizards," Robert Hallbauer and David Thompson, relaxed in the soft leather chairs of the elder Keevil's comfortably sumptuous office. Earlier that afternoon, the Keevils' Teck Corp. had closed a deal taking over Cominco Ltd., a Canadian mining industry giant with assets four times larger than Teck's. The Cominco acquisition capped 32 years of hard-driving growth — a growth that has made Teck, with a book value of $489 million in 1985, the fastest growing mining company in Canada. Along the way, Teck's growth has also made both Keevils wealthy and earned them the reputation of being the fastest, most successful dealmakers in the Canadian resource field.
>
> The Cominco takeover represented the Keevils working at their legendary best.

From there, I related the takeover details and then faded back to when Keevil Sr. created the company.

Starting with the takeover allowed me to establish Keevil as a giant killer. It also permitted me to introduce the other major players in the story — the son and the two "wizards," as they are known in mining-industry circles. It was a classic fiction technique used here in non-fiction. Take the main characters, put them in a room, and then introduce them one by one, revealing their relationships to each other.

I simply had the characters recreate the scene for me. I had been in the office and knew what it looked like. Keevil Sr. told me about the Dom Pérignon and how they sat back and celebrated their victory that day. Those few details brought the introduction to life far more dramatically than if I had merely recounted that on a particular day, Teck Corp. took over Cominco. The scene provided a backdrop against which potentially dull statistical monetary details came to life as vital links to the dealmakers behind the legend.

Pick up almost any magazine and read a few opening paragraphs. Time and time again a scene is created around a person, place, or issue. In travel pieces and community profiles, the writer usually begins with a broad sweep of the area or one symbolic feature. I used this ploy in a profile of the northern Canadian city, Whitehorse. I wanted to write about why anyone would live there, what they worked at, what they spent their money on, and how they played. I needed to create a physical picture of the city. I began:

> Whitehorse's usually clear winter sky has been obscured for nearly a week by heavy cloud. An icy wind whips up off the wide, gray Yukon River, biting exposed skin and persistently worming through coat flaps. A thin layer of snow, crunchy underfoot, blankets the street and square, blocky buildings of downtown. The studded tires of compact cars and four-wheel-drive pickups slither across sheet ice concentrated at intersections. The few pedestrians hasten from doorway to doorway. Most wear heavy, calf-length Yukon Parkas with the fur-cowled hoods up. The parkas' bright colors are dulled by the dusklike light. To the east and west, steep cliffs sweep up to wall the downtown in between gray escarpments. Normally visible beyond them are the mountain peaks that form

Whitehorse's horizon. Today, they are shrouded by the over-hang of cloud. It is a gloomy November day carrying the promise of the long, dark, cold winter still to come, when it can be light for little more than three hours a day and the temperature may plunge below –40 degrees F. for stretches at a time.

Inside his windowless office, Tony Gonda, Yukon Native Products' general manager and 13-year northern veteran, is explaining why he thinks the largest city north of the 60th parallel is, despite the weather, the high costs and the isolation, one of the best places a man can live.

This is the classic wide-angle camera opening you see in many movies. Scan the city in broad strokes and then zoom in on Tony Gonda defending his choice. I concentrate on the bleak aspects because I want the readers to wonder, "God, I'm cold and depressed. How do those northerners stand it?" From there, where Tony jolts them by saying it's one of the best places to live, I go on to tell readers how they do it.

This brings me to the last point I want to make about introductions. Always open a question in the reader's mind. The pennystock piece asked: How does Izzie do it? The Keevils: What's the secret behind the legend? Whitehorse: Why would anyone choose to live there?

Raise the question in the introduction and then answer it in the remainder of the story.

What a Body!

Like all things physical, your article's body is the sum of its parts. If the parts don't fit neatly, the article won't work. It'll stagger when it should glide; fumble when it should catch. Transitions, your article's muscles and bones, link those parts together.

Able-bodied transitions carry you smoothly from point A to B. The transfer from one anecdote or detail to the next should be so slick it goes unnoticed by the reader. Awkward transitions force readers to pause in their reading to orient themselves, as in this example: " '. . . ,' said Bill Jones, as he stared at the bleak grey prison walls of his solitary-confinement cell.

Abigail Schwartz, prison warden, says prisons are a nice place for meeting people with diverse skills."

There's a switch here between characters with no logical connector. The outgoing image should be smoothly linked to the incoming one: " ' . . . ,' said Bill Jones, as he stared at the bleak grey prison walls of his solitary-confinement cell. Despite the stark reality Jones faces, Abigail Schwartz, prison warden, says he will have the opportunity to meet people with diverse skills once he gets out of solitary." Now Abigail can blather on all she wants and the reader is prepared for her viewpoint. Thanks to a star transition.

Remember Keevil Sr.? I handled the transition from the opening material on the corporate takeover to the early days of Keevil's career this way: "A month after the takeover, it was obvious that the fast-moving Keevils were in control and Cominco would be run according to their style. The Teck style began emerging shortly after Keevil Sr., a 15-year geophysics researcher and veteran professor at both Harvard University and the University of Toronto, decided in the 40s to set up a sideline consulting firm."

Two very different points of reference are connected through a discussion of style. Not all transitions shift from major scene to major scene. Some link paragraph to paragraph in what often seems a word dance. How well you perform this dance determines to a large extent your success as a writer.

And there's more to this soft-shoe routine. You can't dance without a rhythm. (Notice the transition here by means of the dance metaphor.)

Rhythm is established by the voice of the writer, suggesting his attitude towards the magazine article. It may be sarcastic, adoring, bored, enthralled, or deliberately neutral. This tone should also suit the subject matter. Pleasant words and short, sprightly sentences are unlikely in an article on terrorist slaughter attacks at airports. Conversely, long sentences loaded with Latinates would jar in a piece on how to hold the perfect child's birthday party. "It is imperative that all sibling rivals be restrained from emotionally or physically competing for the attention of the party participants" would be out of step with the article's topic.

Your rhythm is determined by the magazine's style and your own feelings. Sometimes it's a difficult duet. I once wrote an article for a conservative business magazine on one of British Columbia's fabled entrepreneurs. The magazine wanted articles for a new department that would tell it like it is and give readers insight into the nation's business leaders.

In researching the article, I discovered the entrepreneur was, to put it simply, a jerk. He was rude, arrogant, and uncaring about his employees, and yet he masked it all behind a winning smile and a public persona that belied the reality. I wrote a piece sardonic in voice. It was, I think, one of the best articles I've written. It told the truth without giving any cause for a lawsuit against me or the magazine. More, it exposed the subject through example rather than criticism.

Well, I should have remembered that, despite the editor's liberal claims, it was a conservative magazine. A few months later my article appeared, sanitized beyond recognition. So always keep the magazine in mind and try, while remaining true to yourself, to follow the publication's style and rhythm.

Increasingly, that style includes the writer as an active participant in the article. What used to be literally anathema in non-fiction writing is commonplace today. Survey some popular magazines and undoubtedly you'll notice the writers are right in there with "I" comments scattered throughout, especially in profiles, travel pieces, and investigative journalism.

This trend of "writer as character" creates an atmosphere of immediacy. It provides a ready method for generating vivid scenes. With my newspaper background I resisted this trend for several years but eventually recognized its power to develop a story and provide engaging insights into characters and places.

At the same time, this method has a large pitfall. It is all too easy for the writer to hog the show, aspiring to celebrity status. While this might work for Hunter S. Thompson,

P.J. O'Rourke, and Tom Wolfe, centre stage should be approached warily by any writer not yet transformed from keyboard puncher to media darling. Don't be shy about including yourself in the article if it's appropriate. However, be realistic about your importance to the story and ensure the magazine's style warrants such a personal touch.

Follow, also, these more or less universal article conventions:

- In most cases, use a source's first and last names in initial quotations, then last name only in following citations.
- Use "says" rather than exclaimed, uttered, or other variations, unless the remark calls for added emphasis. Occasionally, you can replace "Jones says" with "says Jones." Use the present tense rather than "said."
- Use active rather than passive language. "Garp bit the dog," rather than "The dog was bitten by Garp."
- Prevent a monotone rhythm by mixing sentences and paragraphs of different lengths. A couple of short sentences, then a long one; a short paragraph followed by a long one.
- Don't add sub-heads unless the article is exceptionally long or the magazine is noted for them. Editors usually write their own sub-heads.
- Don't include bibliographical material within the text or use footnotes for any but scholarly markets. Rather, write something like: "A government report entitled 'Keys to Surviving the Latest Tax Law Changes' warns . . ." Append a copy of the report for the editor and fact checker. And, of course, quote sparingly. Interviews provide the best material, not books and reports.
- Avoid long strings of quotes unbroken by any narrative passages. Long quotes are best summarized, with snippets of the subject's voice tossed in. A long monologue by Keevil Sr. about his son's recalcitrant nature and possessions was reduced to: " So it is up to Keevil Sr. to fill in some of the gaps. His son's house, he says, is in the Point Grey area and is 'a very nice place, too. It also has an indoor pool and a hot greenhouse,' where Keevil Jr., uncharacteristically, grows orchids."

If I'd quoted Keevil Sr. verbatim, the passage would have run longer than the article's entire word count. And I couldn't have slipped in the apparent personality contradiction about the orchids because Keevil Sr. didn't find them an odd hobby for his son.

Keep these points in mind, cover everything you've been assigned, hit on the unexpected truths garnered from your research, and eventually you arrive at the article's conclusion. You now need to tie up loose ends and leave the reader feeling satisfied. Endings, like introductions, have great bearing on your article's reception by editor and reader alike.

Ending in Style

Your conclusion should maintain the rhythm you've established throughout the article and reward the reader with a sense of completion. Usually, this is achieved by creating another strong image, as you did in the introduction. In fact, a common technique is to circle back and tie into the opening scene. The circle is one of the oldest and most successful tricks in magazine writing. My Whitehorse article is a perfect example.

We started on the street on a gloomy winter day with people hurriedly seeking shelter and then cut to Tony Gonda's office to hear about the good life. More details on the reality of living in Canada's far north and then we're back on the street.

> Outside Gonda's office, the wind tears a hole in the thick cloud overhead, allowing a weak glow of afternoon sunlight to wash the town. For a brief moment, the color brightens on the pedestrians' Yukon Parkas, the sheet ice at the intersections gleams sharply and the snow on the escarpment cliff tints a soft pink. In that moment, almost everyone on the street pauses and turns toward the glow. Then the clouds close back in, casting the town into the soft gloom of rapidly approaching twilight, and the people of Whitehorse continue on their way.

Compare the introduction and conclusion. My gloomy opening scene became a concluding visual symbol of Whitehorse optimism. Returning to the opening and examining it with new insights from the body of the article brings the reader full circle.

Another successful ploy is to wrap up the article with an opposing view or anecdote. This works well in how-tos. In the pennystock piece, I began with a player who always wins. I ended with my own dismal foray into the pennystock market. I took a beating. But the article was about gambling and gamblers always holding hope in their hands, so it seemed appropriate to finish thus: "I was among the featureless 85 percent who constitute the penny-stock losers. Like Vegas or Atlantic City losers, we stay quiet about our luck. Let the winners, like Izzie Rotterman, boast. Still, if I happen into a stray $25,000 someday, maybe I'll get Izzie to handle my account. After all, if 15 out of 100 win, doesn't that make the odds about six to one? Not bad for a gambler."

A final trick, if you can't use the circle or opposite techniques, is to come up with an anecdote, analogy, or telling comment that effectively sums up your story. In a profile of a guitar builder, Louise describes the dedication that took him from a chance encounter with classical guitar in Spain to the flawless execution of his craft. Her last lines read: " 'Building guitars sounds so romantic,' says Thompson. 'But it's dirty. It's dusty. It's hard work. It's not romantic at all.' " And then she ends the story with this: "Sorry, Ted. We think you're smitten."

More often than not, you discover the logical conclusion before you write the article. The perfect quote pops up in an interview, research unearths a succinct resolution. But if a finale proves elusive, remember the fail-proof techniques: circle back, opposition, or tidy summation.

All that remains is to edit for grammatical errors, fix up any transitional problems, and make the necessary cuts to meet word count. Then follow Louise's advice in the upcoming chapter to format your well-crafted article into a professional-looking manuscript.

CHAPTER
SEVEN

Looking Like a Pro

First impressions count. Working from the boonies, it's unlikely we'll meet many editors in person so we can't rely on a dress-for-success wardrobe or a firm handshake to establish our professionalism. It's our writing, along with our manuscript presentation and, to a lesser degree, our office equipment, that speaks for us.

Undoubtably, some brilliant writers have had their work accepted scrawled in crayon on the back of a paper bag. For the rest of us, following the industry's standard procedures provides a running start in a competitive business.

Looks Good on Paper

Start with a clean, easy-to-read manuscript. Follow the advice for query letters: twenty-pound white bond paper (letterhead is fine for queries but use plain paper for manuscripts) and clear black type.

On the first page of your manuscript put your name, address, and telephone number (including area code) single-spaced at the top of the left-hand corner. In the top right-hand corner, list the rights you are selling (e.g., First North American serial rights) and the number of words rounded off to the nearest fifty (1,250 words rather than 1,263). Then drop down several inches and type in the article's title. I capitalize and underline mine. Leave four lines and begin your first paragraph, indented five spaces from the left margin. Double-space the remainder of your manuscript. This makes it easy to read and allows the editor room to make changes. If you are writing under another name, put your real name at the top (for the cheque!) and your pen-name after the title. Like this:

```
The Marital Art of Seduction
by Wanda Stiletto
```

There is latitude in how you set up your first page. I keep my title flush with the left margin. Mark likes to centre his. I push my story down the page so there's just room enough for the lead paragraph. Some writers prefer to begin their manuscript a set number of inches from the top.

The following pages of your manuscript require, in either top corner, your last name, the page number, and a slug. A slug is a word, usually pulled from the title, that identifies your article. If you have two manuscripts in an editor's office and they get mixed together, the slug makes it easy to sort them. My second page looks like this:

```
Donnelly/2
Seduction
```

Mark's looks like this:

```
Zuehlke
Tyson
Page 2
```

From the second page onward allow about 250 words per page. (I type twenty-three sixty-character lines). A generous one-inch margin on all four sides is recommended. On the last, page type in "–30–", a typesetter's symbol for "the end", a few lines below the last paragraph. Both Mark and I centre this. Keeping these guidelines in mind, set up your pages in a form you find aesthetically pleasing; it's not necessary to do exactly as we do.

If you're using fanfold paper, remove the feeder tape and separate the pages. Don't leave this chore for the editor.

Proof your manuscript one last time. Neatly correct typos on the page. Retype if you have more than three per page.

Finally, assemble your manuscript in sequence and secure it with a paper clip. Editors like a loose manuscript, so don't be tempted to staple or use a folder or binder.

Fact-Checker List

Many of the larger magazines employ fact checkers to verify the accuracy of your story. Fact checkers are invaluable to writers. Often immensely knowledgeable, they catch errors and ambiguities before they have a chance to embarrass us. Their job is not to polish a hastily researched and poorly written article but to ensure the magazine prints an accurate story. To assist them, enclose a fact-checker list with your manuscript.

To make it easy for the fact checkers, who are often free-lancers working from their homes, to contact you, put your name, address, and phone number at the top of the page. They need to call you if they turn up any discrepancies. List the story's title and the names and phone numbers of all the people you contacted for the article. Include anyone who provided background material or quotes, whether they are named in the article or not. Note beside the contacts' names whether they can only be reached at certain times. Warn the checker if you suspect one of your contacts will be rude or uncooperative. The checker and you both have the same goal: to ensure the story is at its best before publication. Also enclose photocopies of printed research material. (Mark has more on fact checkers in the next chapter.)

Cutline List

If you provide photographs for your article, you need to include cutlines. These are the captions appearing under the photographs. Writing cutlines is a pesky task. It provides, however, a chance to work in a worthy snippet of information you couldn't include in the article. I liked the following quote but didn't have room for it in a piece about an artists' manager, so I used it in the cutline for his photo: " 'I'm an artist, I just don't paint,' says Allen Arndt, the impresario behind the Western Lights Artists Group. To him, art is music made visible." You can also pull an appropriate sentence from your story. To identify a shot of a restaurant's popular dessert, perhaps this: "A fall harvest of Italian plums, slit to reveal their golden flesh and baked under a blanket of sugared almonds, tops the list of The Purple Plum's most frequently requested desserts."

Again, I put my name, address, phone number, and the article's title on my cutline list. The editor sends this along with your photos to the art director. I identify the photos and provide cutlines like this:

> <u>Exterior of restaurant shot</u>: Once again, The Purple Plum rang up four dollar signs in this year's <u>Restaurants You Can't Afford</u>.

> <u>Man with women shot</u>: Employee relations have always been a problem at The Purple Plum. From left to right: Owner Jean de Snoot and staff members Debbie Darling and Lucretia Borgia. (Note: The woman with the rolling pin is Lucretia.)

In group photos name the people from left to right. Then provide additional identification, such as Lucretia's rolling pin. The magazine won't print these notes; they're just to ensure that the person setting up the illustrations for your story gets the names in the correct order.

Put your name and address on your slides and slip them into a slide protector, a plastic sheet with twelve pockets available at photo supply shops. Staple the sheet to your cutline list. If I'm sending prints, I pop them into individual stationery envelopes (with the photo's identification typed on the front). Staple the envelopes to the cutline list. After publication, the magazine returns your photos at their expense.

Invoices

You can buy preprinted forms but it's easy to make an invoice. Type name, address, and phone number at the top of the page. If you're registered, also list your Goods and Services Tax (GST) number. (The next section discusses registering for GST and how GST affects invoicing.) Then type the date and the name and address of the magazine buying your story. Itemize the article and photography fees and any agreed-upon expenses. (Include photocopies of expense receipts.) If you're charging GST, list this amount last. If you're not registered, mark your invoice "Small Supplier" and do not charge the magazine any GST. Note the rights you are selling and, near the bottom of your form, type in the word "Invoice."

Often, you invoice the magazine for the article fee before your telephone bill arrives. When this happens, note "Long-distance expenses to follow" on your invoice. When your phone bill arrives, send off a photocopy with calls billable to the magazine circled. Include a second invoice charging the magazine for long-distance calls, plus its share of any taxes.

The Dreaded GST

It appears the Goods and Services Tax is here to stay. If your gross annual writing income is more than $30,000, you must register with Revenue Canada. Registered writers should follow these guidelines when preparing their invoices: When billing magazines for small amounts (under $30, as I write), the date and amount owing are required. For amounts between $30 and $50, include the date, your name or company name, your nine-digit registration number, amount owing, and a separate listing of GST owing. For amounts exceeding $150, also include the magazine's name, terms of sale (cash; writers don't usually offer credit terms), and a brief description of the service (name of the article).

At required intervals, submit to the government GST you have collected minus GST you've paid out on expenses. Claim a rebate if you've paid out more than you've collected. Appropriate forms are issued by Revenue Canada.

If you earn under $30,000, you are not required to register with the federal government. Simply mark your invoices "Small Supplier" and do not charge the magazine GST. Then, however, you are not eligible for reimbursement of any GST paid out on your expenses. For this reason, many writers with modest incomes are registering. A current bulletin from Revenue Canada can help you decide if registration might benefit you.

Cover Letter

Many writers like to include a cover letter with their manuscript. It's another opportunity for us boonie writers to establish rapport with our editors. It can be a short note saying, "Here's the Purple Plum story. I hope I never see another plum, but the piece was fun to research. I'm looking forward to seeing it in print." It can also be a chance to strike while the iron is hot. I try to include a suggestion for another story whenever I mail off a manuscript. It tells editors I'm a prolific writer and thinking of their magazine. I add a postscript to my cover letter: "I've also enclosed an idea for the summer issue. Let me know what you think." Then I include a query letter pitching the idea.

Now you're ready to bundle everything off to the magazine. Use a strong manila envelope large enough to mail your work flat, and address it to the magazine, attention your editor. Stack up your cover letter, manuscript, fact-checker list, cutline list with photos, and invoice with expense receipts and slip all this, along with a sturdy piece of cardboard to protect your photos, in the envelope. If I'm suggesting another story, I include a SASE. Apply sufficient postage, say a short prayer if you're so inclined, then kiss it goodbye.

Say Cheese

Photography is my least favourite aspect of magazine writing. The large-circulation magazines assign their own photographers but many smaller magazines expect writers to provide photos. If you enjoy photography, you can combine it with writing for a wonderful career, like several outdoor writers I know. They wouldn't think of going anywhere without their trusty camera equipment. Me, I had to be coerced into taking my camera to Hawaii. Even though I'm not fond of photography, I have picked up some bare-bones tips which I'll pass on to you. For more information, inquire at your local camera shop. There are dozens of excellent books available, as well as classes and workshops.

I've got by with an older 35-mm Pentax single-lens reflex camera with a 50-mm lens and a battery-operated electronic flash unit (both belonging to my husband). The 50-mm lens is standard with most cameras and is a good multi-purpose lens. Eventually you may want to add a 105-mm lens. It lets you maintain a little distance from your subjects but still get a close-up shot. Mark likes this one for scenic shots, too. A 28-mm lens with its wider angle is nice for interior shots of rooms and businesses.

Pick a flash unit that swivels. This allows you to bounce its light off a ceiling or wall. A flash aimed directly at the subject often results in a photo with a bleached-out foreground, harsh shadows, and red eyes.

Become familiar with your camera equipment. On assignment is not the time to realize you don't know how to operate your flash. Build your confidence by practising on friends or even the family dog. Always carry extra film and fresh batteries. Keep your equipment together and you won't forget anything in a last-minute rush. (I keep mine, along with my tape recorder and notepad, in a sturdy leather tote.)

People are uncomfortable having their pictures taken. I find they're more relaxed after the interview, and that's usually when I take my photographs. I try to have them hold onto something, a stair railing, the back of a chair, their product. Having something to do with their hands puts them more at ease and their composure shows in the photos. To ensure I have some good pictures, I take as many shots as my subject's patience allows and I bracket them. This means that I first use the light metre's indicated exposure. Then I shoot additional exposures, both over and under, to compensate for difficult light situations. To facilitate the magazine's layout, take both vertical and horizontal shots.

Most magazines want colour slides. The occasional magazine requests a print. Rather than switching films, I use slide film and have a print made from the slide. It's much easier to store slides and they hold up better over time than prints and negatives. Some slide films must be processed at special labs. Others can be developed overnight at a local shop. If you have a tight deadline or (heaven forbid) you have to reshoot because of technical problems, use a film your local shop can process.

Newspapers, and some magazines, request black-and-white photos. Again, I recommend using a film that can be developed locally.

When writers are required to provide photos with their stories, they can, occasionally, with the editor's prior approval, get out of actually taking the pictures themselves. Many subjects offer their own photos. Artists, in particular, often have excellent shots of their work. Tourist attractions, businesses, community associations, and government agencies usually have access to good photos. Newspapers often sell photos for a photo credit and a moderate fee.

Looking Like a Pro

Magazine writing is a relatively cheap business to enter. If you have a generous friend (or spouse) you might get away without buying a camera. And simply having access to a typewriter, when you're still feeling out article writing, will get you started. Soon, though, it becomes impractical to borrow one or pay a service to type your queries and manuscripts. Then it's time to buy your own equipment, equipment that demonstrates your commitment to writing.

Most editors still accept typewritten manuscripts, although there may come a time when magazines require that all articles be submitted on computer disk. If you're using a typewriter and run into this situation, a word-processing service can make a disk for you.

Should you decide not to purchase a computer initially, try to choose a typewriter with the larger pica type (ten characters per inch) over the smaller élite (twelve per inch). Use a clean, simple typeface, not script, so your words are easy to read. I started out using a portable electric typewriter with correctable ribbon, which was handy, as I'm not the world's best typist. In fact, that was why, two years later, I invested in a computer.

It wasn't love at first sight. For the first few days I hated my computer. Had I just wasted several months' worth of hard-earned cash? I couldn't make it do anything the manual said it should. In the end, I paid for two hours with a computer technician who showed me everything I needed to know to produce manuscripts that looked like those I had been typing. I was smitten (with the computer). The technician was hardly out of my driveway before I was keyboarding in an article I had been working up on my typewriter. I've never looked back.

My computer allows me to move words and paragraphs effortlessly, so I don't hesitate to edit my work. I also find the words flow easier than when I use a typewriter. (I've never been able to write longhand. I have terrible penmanship and my thoughts are always faster than my hand.) The computer keyboard is also a lot less fatiguing than a typewriter's. And it's easy to make copies of your work. But the most satisfying benefit is letter-perfect manuscripts. No sooner would I pull a page from the typewriter than I'd spot two or three typos. Now, a few corrective strokes on the computer's keyboard yield pristine copy.

There is so much information available on computers it's overwhelming. Writers' needs are quite simple. We need enough computer memory (measured in kilobytes) to accommodate our word-processing program, operating system, several articles, and perhaps a book-length manuscript. (You never know where your writing will lead!) Look for 512K or 640K. When I shopped around even moderately priced systems were offering 512K.

Mark uses a dual-drive floppy system. My computer has a hard drive. That just means I can store more information in my computer than Mark can. He keeps his articles or book chapters on disks and feeds them into the computer when he's ready to work on them. I can simply turn on my computer and call up my work immediately (although I copy all my work onto disks for safekeeping in case my hard drive "crashes" and loses all my writing). Hard-drive storage capacity is measured in "megabytes" (one million bytes); twenty megabytes, which

I have, is sufficient for most writers. Room for lots of writing, but not so large that it takes forever to copy your stored work onto backup disks.

Choosing the right word-processing program is important. You can saturate yourself with information on various software and, if you're like me, still not know which one is right for you. I knew I wouldn't know what I wanted in a program until I had worked with my computer for awhile. Salespeople in computer stores can offer advice but may not understand the needs of a professional writer. You need a program that allows you to delete, move, and copy blocks of text; insert or overwrite text; and produce a manuscript similar to those you've been typing — all quickly and efficiently. A spellchecker is optional — neither Mark nor I use one, although some writers swear by them.

Your best bet is to get a recommendation from another writer, not always easy in the boonies. I've been very happy with Mark's suggestion, PC-Write by Quicksoft.

Next to the word-processing program, the printer is probably your most important decision. Pick one that produces a manuscript that's clear and easy to read. There are four basic types of printers: Dot-matrix, daisy-wheel, ink jet and laser. The last three can be pricey. Dot-matrix printers are relatively inexpensive and can produce acceptable copy. The print quality depends on the number of pins (more pins print smaller dots closer together, making darker print). Mark has a nine-pin printer and it produces good copy. Mine has twenty-four, so it is a little sharper.

I've been told it's a good idea to pick out your word-processing program and your printer first, then choose a computer that meets their operational requirements. It can help narrow down a bewildering choice of units.

You may also want a modem. This device sends and receives computer data via the telephone. It allows you to tap into data-base services and to speedily transmit your manuscripts to magazines set up to receive copy by modem. Magazines facing tight deadlines, however, are relying more on fax machines. These machines are still costly to buy, but many office-supply stores provide fax service for a fee. If the magazine requests your manuscript by fax, bill them for the transmission costs.

Early in your career, you need to invest in a telephone answering machine. Editors may call while you're out and they don't have time for repeat calls. Before I had one, an editor wrote saying she would have assigned a story if she could have reached me by phone. Needless to say, I bought an answering machine the next day. I had just plugged it in when another editor called to give me an assignment (which more than paid for the machine) and ask if I would also write a monthly column for the magazine.

Choose an answering machine that allows you to record telephone conversations, a handy feature for over-the-phone interviews. Always use a brief and straightforward outgoing message. Elaborate or corny announcements don't enhance your professional image.

You also need a portable tape recorder. I was already lugging around my camera equipment, so I wanted a small recorder. I chose a palm-sized one with good sound. It does have a few drawbacks, however. It uses micro-cassettes, only thirty minutes per side and more expensive than regular cassettes, and it gives no signal when the tape has expired. I recommend buying one that makes an audible click when you reach the end of the tape.

The last purchase I'm going to talk about is one you should make as soon as you're serious about writing. It's stationery — or, at the very least, business cards. A good business card makes you look professional. And it gives you something to hand out to contacts, potential clients, and your interview subjects. It should include your mailing address with country and telephone with area code. My card is white with dark blue lettering and identifies me simply as writer. Mark's is cream with brown lettering with the inscription "freelance writer". Either designation is fine. If you market photos, editing, or consulting services, your card should mention that as well.

Later you may add letterhead, envelopes, or both. I use plain paper with my card paper-clipped to the right-hand corner for queries and letters. Mark has letterhead. He uses plain envelopes and rubber-stamps his address. I have personalized envelopes.

Feeling Like a Pro

At the start, you can get by working on the kitchen table or in a corner of the bedroom or living room. There comes a time, though, when you outgrow this space and long for a "real" office. Some writers actually rent office space. For most of us, however, one appeal of freelancing is the opportunity to work from home. But no matter where you set up your office, you need a place where you can direct your energy towards writing, not hunting for lost files, missing notes, or an elusive address book.

I am lucky. I have a spare room in my house. Even starting out with an old kitchen chair, the top of a dresser, and my typewriter balanced on a piece of plyboard, I had a place to work efficiently. I filed my notes in recycled junk-mail envelopes stored in cardboard boxes. My telephone and answering machine were at hand. If an editor called, I could find any paperwork in seconds.

Now I have a beautiful office. One that's not only efficient, but comfortable and a joy to work in. Good lighting, a steno chair with back support, lots of shelves for books and magazines, an oak-trimmed work space for my computer system, and a real filing cabinet.

Mark is fortunate to have a spare room, too. His teak-fitted office opens onto a small sundeck. He can edit his work out in our famous Okanagan Valley sunshine just steps away from the telephone and his files.

Our offices are where we labour, five or more days a week. We have created an environment that allows us to give our best to our chosen career. To clients, interview subjects, or casual visitors, these rooms say, "This is where a writer works." More importantly, though, our offices are an affirmation to ourselves of our worth as writers. We are professionals and we rate a professional workplace.

CHAPTER EIGHT

The Winding Road

You have a professionally prepared article in the mail well before your first assignment's deadline. Contented but battle weary, you lean back in your chair to ponder the future and bask in the glow of success. How marvellous it will be to see your first boldly inked byline glistening out at the world from a glossy page. You will be vindicated before all those who seemed to think your desire to write for magazines was a pleasant fantasy best left in the realm of daydreams. Yes, you are now a writer. When the magazine publishes your piece, that will be a reality plain to all.

The publication of your first article is an exciting moment in your writing career, but remember that is all it is — a moment. Before you stretches a road likely to include hundreds of articles for scores of magazines. You always remember that first article more keenly than most (many you forget and some you desperately want to forget), but it is only a starting point. It is time to get on with the future.

Start tracking down more assignments and assessing other writing opportunities. Having established a toehold on the shores of the magazine industry, the task now is to widen that tenuous perch into a firm beachhead and begin the push inland that eventually confirms your position as a seasoned veteran. Pursuing the advancement of your career with aggressive enthusiasm, you find thoughts of the finished article seldom occur. Meantime, of course, the article is in the hands of editors. The day is bound to come when the phone rings and you find that article suddenly thrust back into the limelight as the editor clamours for your immediate attention to what may seem to you by now little more than a fond memory.

This unexpected interruption can seem rather bothersome and regressive, the first time it happens. After all, how many months ago did you write that article? And now they want you to tinker with it? What you are about to experience is the afterworld of magazine writing — the simple fact that even long after you have been paid by the magazine, the article continues down the road towards the date of its publication. And as it makes that passage, you will quite possibly be called upon many times to help it complete the journey.

The Road to Print

When Paul McCartney and John Lennon wrote "The Long and Winding Road," they could have been talking of the process articles go through in reaching print. The twists and turns facing your prose vary greatly from one magazine to another, and depend to a large degree on the editors' and publishers' personal roadmap. Your role in getting your creation to that final destination also depends much on the whim of editorial policy.

There are no rules governing the degree of a writer's involvement after an article has been submitted for publication. Some magazines ask for repeated rewrites, or call upon you to confirm fact-checking reports or read and approve galleys; some even seek your vision of how the article should be illustrated. Others simply take the article, pay you, and at a later date print it with no further contact between you and the editor. Still others may do all of the above and throw in a few middle-ground variations as well.

Luckily, there are certain magazine industry tendencies that help you determine each article's likely route. The size of a magazine's budget and staff has a lot to do with its probable approach to your article.

If the magazine is small, it probably leans towards the "send cheque and print without further ado" end of the scale. Small magazines usually have harried, underpaid editors with little time to spend reworking articles, checking facts, or soliciting writer's opinions on final presentation of material. They are usually just too busy trying to keep ahead of the relentless cycle of publishing deadlines.

In one way, these are the easiest magazines to work for; they can also be the most frustrating. On the plus side, you are unlikely to find yourself doing much rewriting, fielding seemingly trivial questions the editors could have answered themselves, or wading line by line through galley proofs to ensure accuracy. Processing an article from manuscript to print can be tedious, and these editors spare you.

But serious problems can arise from this early exclusion. When the article comes out in print with your byline, you may wish it hadn't. As a case in point, I wrote in my newspaper days a court piece on a trial of three Sikh males charged with the aggravated assault of another Sikh. I scrupulously recorded the spelling of each defendant's name and, while writing the article, painstakingly ensured each was correctly spelled throughout. I then went back to court.

In the morning, I blearily (newspaper reporters always read the paper blearily) scanned the article and was surprised to learn there must have been at least a dozen different defendants in the Sikh assault case. It was as if the typesetter had taken a crack at each name after putting on a blindfold. Had I been able to proof a galley of the article, I could have headed the whole thing off by making corrections.

While this particular fiasco resulted from sloppy typesetting, many others result from editorial caprice. Editors sometimes change copy with the best of intentions. They may want to tighten a sloppy sentence. Or perhaps they just want to jazz up the writing, fit it more closely to the magazine's style, or cut the length. There are also editors who feel everything crossing their desk must be edited regardless of need. Whatever the motive, chances abound for the meaning of things to get twisted beyond recognition.

Even worse, if your name, like mine, is difficult to spell and you don't get to see a galley proof, your article comes out with your moniker misspelled. This will haunt you. Instead of the article appearing under your name listing in the *Canadian*

Periodical Indexes and other such guides, a ghost personality dogs along beside you just a column or so over on the page.

At the other end of the spectrum are magazines wanting your participation in bringing the article to print. These are often larger-circulation, higher-paying, glossier productions. They expect your help in delivering the best possible product.

First, they look for excellent writing up front and frown upon you if your submission was hastily written, sloppily researched, or technically flawed, or if you missed the deadline. But even if the article sparkled with creative excellence, resonated with informative authority, and was a pearl of presentation and punctuality, you still won't be home free.

In the first few weeks, expect only silence. Your manuscript slumbers amid a pile of soon-to-be-reads. Occasionally, editors give your piece a quick read and call to say they've received it, liked it, and are cutting a cheque. But don't hold your breath waiting for reaction. Usually you hear from the editors only after they've had time to read the article thoroughly and determine their response.

Finally, however, the day arrives when the phone rings or you receive a package in the mail. Expect the following. Assuming you have done your initial research, writing, and manuscript preparation well, the first thing you hear is that the editor liked the article and everything seems on track. Your payment has been processed, expenses forwarded to accounts. Just as you start to relax and savour success, you hear something like, "I've just got a few questions."

Starting on the first page, the editor proceeds to go line by line through your manuscript asking you to explain something here, expand something there, get a more definite quote on this point, tighten up that paragraph, provide a bit more colour in this scene, and finally rewrite the conclusion so it underscores the article's central premise. "Oh, and we're running a little behind, so do you think you could have this done by tomorrow, the next day at the latest?" Hiding your dismay, you affirm this is manageable.

Hanging up, you stare at the handwritten notes crabbed all over your manuscript. Probably you find you need to make several follow-up research calls to sources to plumb new depths missed initially. Some of the editor's wish list requires major reworking of paragraphs. And after you make all these changes, the word count often balloons to gargantuan proportions. So even the paragraphs the editor left untouched suddenly must be placed under the microscope of revision, as you conduct delicate microsurgery on your article to save the word count.

You persevere, however, get the rewrite done on time, and send it back to the editor. This time, the response is likely to be more immediate. Expect at least a few more questions about the new details. Don't be surprised if you even end up doing some rewriting on the phone at this stage as you and the editor struggle to get the image perfect.

At times during the rewriting phase, you truly marvel at the insight and vision of your editor. Other times, you wonder at the person's utter lack of mental capability. "Of course that's what I meant," you may want to scream. Don't. The editor is doing a good job, at such times, by not passing over something that might be hazy enough to take on unintended meaning in the reader's mind.

Editors who demand extensive rewriting are usually the best in the business. They are dedicated to excellence and to clarity of communication. If you listen to them, and listen well, they can teach you vast amounts about writing for magazines and cut years off your learning curve. In time, you will find yourself becoming more critical of your own writing and avoiding earlier errors. Even then, however, expect to rewrite. For major magazines, it's a rare article that requires no revision.

Most rewrites are justified, logical, and in line with your original assignment. A few are not. In these cases, you may have an editor who wants rewrites that essentially create a new article.

I once wrote a short article on the workplace phenomenon of burnout. In my original assignment discussion with the editor, we agreed the article was too short to make a personal-experience anecdote from a burnout victim the central thread around which the advice on recognizing symptoms, arranging treatment, and adopting preventative strategies should be spun. A few weeks after I submitted it, a different editor phoned to say he wanted a personal-experience anecdote woven into the piece. Additionally, he had some other points that needed clarification. The other matters were reasonable and did not alter the fundamental nature of the article.

Finding and integrating the personal-story angle, however, would have entailed writing virtually a new article. I told the editor I was unwilling to do this without extra pay. While he didn't particularly like my reaction, he did have to concede my point. The personal-anecdote approach was dropped from the rewrite request.

When a rewrite is required, carefully assess whether the work severely alters the article's nature. If you think it does, don't hesitate to discuss this with the editor and seek compensation for the extra work. Never forget that the time you spend on rewrites could be spent developing queries and researching other assignments. Rewrites are a fact of the business, but an editor should not be using them to change the focus of an article.

Neither should editors use rewrites to update an article they allowed to lie around untended for many months. Almost any article has a built-in timeliness. Sometimes editorial imperatives, such as juggling the need for an excess-article inventory against the limits of available publication space, can result in an article losing relevance. This is not your fault. If a rescue is possible, it should be something you are paid to do, not passed back in the guise of a rewrite. Don't be afraid to ask for extra payment if you think it is warranted. Defend your position clearly, firmly, professionally. Usually, the editor will come around. Most editors are harried and overworked, but they are not by nature intentionally unjust. Sometimes they simply need a gentle reminder of what is and is not fair.

How Long Is That Bridge?

By the time the rewriting process is finally completed, anything from six weeks to several months will have passed. Still, you may not have seen the last of your article.

Shortly after you and the editor complete the final revisions, you receive yet another call. This time it will be the magazine's fact checker. Remember how you took the length of a bridge and tied it into the article to add the ring of statistical authority? The figure was in feet and inches in your old encyclopedia, so you did a metric conversion on the calculator and rounded that figure off.

Well, the fact checker has news. Between the printing of your old encyclopaedia and today, an extension ramp was added, your metric converter is obviously on the blink, so the actual bridge length is more than you quoted. At first, this news leaves you unnerved, blushing with shame over your sloppy research. But then you realize the truth — the fact checker has just saved you from being embarrassed in print.

At the best magazines, a fact checker is a professional researcher who, with Sherlock Holmes's scrupulous eye for detail, ensures every sentence is accurate. Some middle-level magazines have their editors fill this role; the smaller magazines are just as likely not to do any fact checking. In the best situation, the fact checker gives your article an additional ring of authority.

If you are working for a magazine that uses a fact checker, here is what you can expect. The checker uses a variety of sources to go through your copy and proof it against any factual errors you or the editor may have made. If you say the carpet of a particular hotel was red, the checker calls the hotel to ensure you're not colour blind. No detail is too insignificant to escape the checker's attention.

The checker also contacts everyone quoted in the article to make sure they were correct in the details they gave you. There is nothing like a second kick at the can to clarify someone's comments or recollection of events.

Checkers are nothing if not a little devious so don't worry that they might read entire quotes to the subjects. To do that would invite a sudden belaboured rewrite as the interviewees realize they were perhaps a little too flip with you, or went further than they might have wished, or didn't sound academic enough. Given the chance, most interview subjects would rewrite their comments to sound like missives from the federal government. If you quote Miranda Jangles saying, "I was twenty-three when I married that worthless slime bucket Mack Stack," what the checker asks Miranda is, "You were twenty-three when you married Mack Stack?"

Good fact checkers are to be prized. Give them all the time they need. Clarify any concerns they have carefully and honestly. If, in their discussions with interview subjects, a point has arisen contradicting your earlier quote, don't be afraid to reassess things in light of this information. Often a subject may have made an error in the initial explanation and a correction only makes the article better. But, if you think the subject is just trying to sound better or backtrack in self-protection, stand by your original quote. The fact checker won't arbitrarily change the quote against your will. The conflicting responses are passed on to the editor and the two of you are left to solve the contradiction.

Journey's End

Finally, when the fact checking is completed and the rewrites done, the article makes its way through typesetting. Many magazines automatically send, for your approval, galley proofs of the final typeset copy. This is an exact version of the article as it will be printed. Be sure to meet their deadline for response. If you are tardy getting back to them, you may find those last-minute typos you discovered go into print anyway. By the galley-proof stage a definite publishing date has been set and is only days, sometimes hours, away.

At this point no factual material should need clarification. What you are watching for in the galley proofs is typesetting errors, transposed paragraphs, misspellings of names, grammatical gaffs, and the like. You are also checking to see that the editor, in a last-minute adjustment of a sentence or paragraph, didn't completely lose the meaning of your original passage.

Compare a galley proof line by line against your final draft, and if you have any corrections, mark them in the margins. If you are unsure how to edit copy, there are any number of guides to copyediting available at bookstores. These contain all the correct symbols and forms you need to know for proofing. When you are done with the corrections, immediately send them back to the editor. If everything is perfect, let the editor know so the article can be moved into the final production process.

The final galley proof is usually the last time you are involved with the article until the day a copy of the magazine comes in the mail. The first time this happens is great. In fact, these moments never lose their appeal. There is something about seeing your article in print, with accompanying art work, that tends to leave a deep sense of accomplishment. Savour it. Then put the article in its file and get on with the next one.

By the time you finally hold that article in your hand, it will be yesterday's news. If you have been diligently working on other projects, the press of new deadlines allows little time for reflection.

And you should have other projects in line because well over a year may have passed. There is no real rhyme or reason to the publication of articles in magazines. Editors face a difficult task when it comes to assigning articles and setting publication dates. All too often, it is like trying to forsee the future through a badly clouded and cracked crystal ball.

Editors usually give out assignments several months before they think the article will be printed. Three to six months seems to be the average timing ratio. The number of articles scheduled for each issue is based on projected advertising sales. Ratios vary, but most magazines dependent on advertising revenue print a page of editorial for every page of advertising sold. Past performance gives the sales department an estimate of what they can expect to sell for each issue.

This information is passed on to the editor who then tries to line up an equivalent amount of editorial copy.

It's all a calculated gamble which often craps out. Sometimes advertising sales take off, leaving an editor desperately short of copy and calling up writers to beg articles on very short deadlines. Sadly, editors more often find they have more copy on file than needed, resulting in print delays.

If your article is delayed, don't worry unduly. It doesn't mean it was the weakest article in the line-up. Editors strive for an eclectic mix and your piece may simply be the wrong spice for this month's menu. Or it may have been too long or too short for the available space. The reasons are as varied as the hair colour of a dozen editors.

Usually the article appears. But occasionally an article is bumped so repeatedly it becomes stale and dated. In this case, it will probably never see print. An article I wrote on the ins and outs of investing in the Canadian fashion industry was rendered meaningless when the stock market crashed and stayed in the doldrums for more than a year. Another article on collecting player pianos lost currency when the column section it was to be included in was cancelled. There was nothing wrong with either story. They were just victims of bad timing. In the end, I was paid for both of them, so there was nothing to do but go on to the next project.

Dollars for Free

Some magazine articles are like volunteer vegetables in a garden; they refuse to wither and die but continue to flourish and produce bumper profits. These articles are truly manna from heaven. If you find yourself in possession of such a proliferous plant, relax, enjoy, deposit the cash. I speak here of articles which yield second-rights sales.

It is because of these articles that you never — unless you are generously rewarded with an outrageously excessive payment for an article and possibly trips to exotic sunspots — agree to sell more than first-time serial rights. Not every article you write will have resale potential, but there are always a few; and often the ones which prove most profitable surprise even the most seasoned second-rights seller.

I, like many magazine writers I know, have never been diligent in seeking out second-rights markets. Although I creatively spin the same research material into several unique articles for non-competitive markets, once the articles are completed I tend to file and forget. This is less for want of entrepreneurial skill than in response to the pressure of time. Vigorously marketing second rights takes time, so most writers don't bother.

But we should. And so should you. So now, like any good general addressing the troops, I'm going to issue commands for you to follow a winning strategy I've never tested. I have, however, listened to the success stories of a number of my more tactically minded veteran colleagues and shall unabashedly reveal their stratagems. (I'm also going to leave this military metaphor behind. Amazing how quickly metaphoric imagery can lose its spark, isn't it? A point worth remembering.)

If you are seriously going to market second rights, the key is to be businesslike. Develop an inventory of the articles you have written, detailing their subject matter and the kind of market to which each will likely appeal. As your bank of articles grows, break them into subject groupings, business articles in one group, fitness in another, equine somewhere else.

Once you have a bank established and a system in place for tracking the articles, start evaluating potential markets. The most vociferous market for second-rights material is *Reader's Digest*, which regularly fills as much as three-quarters of its publication with reprints of previously published material. If you think any of your articles fit their format without paralleling something they've recently published, consider sending them a copy for consideration. Do not send second-rights markets a clipping of the article from the magazine which bought first-serial rights. Rather, send a fresh manuscript copy. If you have a computer this is easy; if not, start making a quality photocopy of each of your articles before shipping it off to the magazine buying first rights, and then use this copy to reproduce second-rights submissions. Otherwise, you're going to have a lot of typing to do and will probably soon lose interest in selling second rights. Include with the article a letter stating that you are offering second rights and note the magazine in which the piece was originally published, giving the month and page numbers. This approach is best for all second-rights sales you initiate.

Reader's Digest and similar publications are the most obvious second-rights markets, but they are not the only ones. And because of their generalist nature they are not a strong market for deeply researched, specialized material. For these markets you will have to dig further into the magazine-publishing industry, not merely scan the publications around a grocery store check-out counter. It is here that various writers' guides to markets can be most useful, particularly such industry bibles as *The Literary Marketplace*, both North American and international editions.

Remember that article you wrote on fly-fishing the Skeena River in northern British Columbia and sold to a provincially based tourist magazine? In your second-rights marketing frame of mind, it now occurs to you that many American outdoor magazines might find that a piece about the joys of standing in icy water up to your waist in hip waders to catch some of the sweetest-tasting trout in the world constitutes a perfect excursion into Canada's north. This decided, make up some copies of your article and photos and pack them off. If you want to keep your marketing costs down, instead of sending the full article write a brief, sharply written synopsis which describes the piece, photos available, and where the article was previously published. Include a SASE if you want to keep track of which magazines reject the offer, or allow them a reasonable time (six weeks is usually sufficient) to reply and if you don't hear from them, assume they are not interested.

You can use the same approaches with international magazines. Many German and Japanese publications, for example, regularly feature travel articles on North American destinations. That fly-fishing hole on the Skeena might again be perfect, especially as it is about doing something, rather than just sightseeing. Increasingly, travel editors are looking for this more active kind of material.

No matter what articles you write, whether oriented towards business, fitness, or hog farming, there will always be publications in other areas of the world with an interest in the facts of life in your corner of the world.

Sometimes the best market for second-rights articles is under your nose. If you write a feature for a major Canadian magazine about a local celebrity or business, consider offering second rights to a magazine published in your area. Although the pay is usually low, it is still money you would not otherwise have, and for it you have to do nothing more than send a copy of the manuscript off in the mail.

Even if you never get around to marketing second rights, or do so only fitfully, chances are you will receive offers to purchase second rights. Most come out of the blue and from an amazingly varied range of markets. In the past few years, I have sold second rights to corporations I have written about that wish to reprint the article for employee newsletters; an American audio-tape company that reproduces business articles on cassettes so that harried businesspeople can furtively monitor the world of business while stuck in traffic jams; educational textbook publishers; and even a cattle rancher who produced a labour-of-love newsletter for other ranchers raising a special breed of cattle.

The bulk of these offers come through referrals from the magazine in which the article originally appeared. When someone contacts a publication to buy second rights, it is routine to refer the interested party directly to the writer. Unless they have purchased all rights from you, magazines do not sell the rights themselves or act on your behalf as go-between.

When I am contacted about second rights, there are a few points I always determine from the buyers. I find out what their interest is, whether they are looking to use it as a corporate promotion piece, whether they are a magazine, or whatever. This helps when it comes to negotiating a fee for the rights. The other matter I determine is what is required of me to make the sale, so I am sure it is a second-rights sale we are talking about and not a rewriting of the article to produce something new. (If it was, I would charge regular rates for this.) I also find out what distribution net the reprinted material will extend into, as this helps in estimating what to charge.

I never allow second-rights use for free. A magazine writer is in business, and if you give something away for free, very shortly it has little or no value. The other thing I never do is allow a second-rights reprint of my article to appear in a non-copyrighted form, as that would jeopardize the future salability of the piece by enabling the unscrupulous to reprint from the non-copyrighted source, circumventing my copyright.

How much do you charge for second rights? Whatever you think you can get. There are, however, a few guidelines that have proved helpful for me and others in this game. Some publications buying second rights have a standard, non-negotiable fee beyond which they won't go. The audio-tape company mentioned earlier is such a case. They pay a flat fee for all the material they use, whether it is a 10,000-word musing from Henry Kissinger first printed in *Business Week*, or a 450-word report on the symptoms of burnout written by myself and published in a small Canadian business journal. But like most second-rights purchasers who contact you, they require absolutely nothing other than permission to run the piece. I write no letter, send no copies of articles, do precisely nothing but endorse and deposit the cheque when it arrives in the mail.

Sometimes the buyer asks for a fee quote. If this happens, don't panic. And certainly don't ask what the buyer is willing to pay and simply take that. The Periodical Writers Association of Canada once conducted an informal poll of members who regularly sold second rights. While the rates differed to some extent, a rule of thumb can be drawn from the results. Most questionnaire respondents took the original fee paid for the piece, divided it by half, and then charged that amount. An article originally selling for $600, then, yields a second-rights sale of $300. This figure, of course, varies somewhat depending on the publication it is to appear in, the money you think they have to spend, and the lifespan the second-rights piece will enjoy. For example, I will charge more to an educational book publisher reprinting an article of mine in a geography text with an initial print run of thirty thousand and an anticipated marketable lifespan of three years than I will to a small trade magazine reaching three thousand sub-scribers with plans to use my article only once. But my base starting point is always half of the original selling price. And usually I get my price.

There is one major exception to this rule. If a company I have written about intends to use my article as a promotional tool, I charge the full rate I was originally paid and usually set a time limit on how long the article can be used before I have to be paid an additional fee. There are two reasons behind this approach. First, I don't go out of my way to en-courage this particular use of my articles as it can raise a few ethical problems in cases where I might have some reserva-tions about the company itself. Secondly, since it's initiating the purchase, the company must see my article as a strong marketing tool. And the fact is, advertising copy is generally better paid, so the company is used to paying higher rates than those common for magazine editorial copy. Finally, I always send a letter of confirmation of the sale with terms of agreement to any company buying second rights for pro-motional use. I produce the letter in duplicate and require them to return a signed copy to me. The agreement should also require the company to forward the material to you in the planned usage format for prior approval. This avoids dis-tortions and editorial changes that could leave you sounding like the company PR person masquerading as a professional journalist who publishes in respected magazines.

There is a new avenue opening that should also result in a flow of money into the pockets of magazine writers for articles they have published. The Canadian Reprography Collective, commonly known as CanCopy, protects the copyright of regis-tered writers from being photocopied and misused by others.

Structured similarly to the Public Lending Rights Commission, which makes annual payments to writers for library use of their books, CanCopy is negotiating usage rights with government, educational institutes, and other mass photocopiers to ensure that writers are compensated fairly for materials copied by these bodies. For example, there has been no compensation paid to writers whose material is photocopied by college instructors and distributed to students as a reading assignment. CanCopy will require that a payment for copying rights be made to the collective, and this fund will then be pooled and paid out under a percentage formula to member writers.

If you become a member of the Periodical Writers Association of Canada, you are automatically included in the collective under a blanket agreement between CanCopy and the Association. Those magazine writers who are not members of PWAC must pay a small annual fee for CanCopy membership. As I write this, CanCopy is still in the establishment phase, but it has signed a number of agreements with various levels of government entailing payments of several million dollars per annum to the collective. The CanCopy pool can only increase as more agreements are reached with other mass-copying bodies. Expectations are that payments to member writers will eventually equal those paid to writers through the Public Lending Rights Commission.

Beyond the Pale

Few writers earn their living exclusively from writing magazine articles. Most combine article writing with other endeavours. The opportunities to earn money from your writing are often limited only by your imagination.

In large urban centres, most magazine writers augment their income by writing for corporations and government. They may write corporate annual shareholder reports, advertising copy, operation and policy manuals, news releases, film scripts, and innumerable other material, all with one central goal in mind: this is material written to make the government or corporate body look good.

While it is undoubtedly easier to land this kind of work when you live in a large urban area, where corporate and government head offices are only minutes away, it is not impossible to find such work in the boonies. In past years, I have written press releases and film scripts for a provincial government ministry, brochures promoting various company products, an opthalmologist's guide to cataract-removal operations, tourism brochures for a provincial tourism ministry, and industrial-development material for local municipal governments.

The trick is to let the local community know you are out there. Circulate your business cards at every opportunity. Consider becoming involved in local clubs, business groups, art organizations and other bodies where you can develop a public presence. Louise is much better at this than I am, as I abhor volunteering and am somewhat reclusive. Through participation in organizations such as Women In Business, Louise has managed to extend her public presence throughout her community with the result that she is often contacted out of the blue with offers of work on various local writing projects.

When you complete a project, be sure to get numerous copies for yourself to show other potential clients. And then mercilessly promote yourself at every opportunity.

Right about now, you are probably thinking that this is all very well, but you have no idea how to write press releases, brochure copy, corporate reports, film scripts, and the like. Well, a little while ago you didn't know much about writing for magazines, either. There is no mystery to any of these types of writing. The best way to learn about them is to pick up books at the library, as well as samples of each type of writing from local and national sources, and study the techniques. Such books as Thomas Bivins's *Handbook for Public Relations Writing* (NTC Business Books, 1989) can show you quickly a great deal of what you need to know to be active in this field.

As with magazines, start putting out feelers within the community for contracts by getting in touch with local companies and government agencies to see what work is available. Leave a brief, one-page profile describing who you are, the types of writing services you offer, and any relevant past experience you have. Think of these as another form of query letter.

When you land work, be sure to charge a professional fee. Check writers' guides, like *The Writer's Market*, to see what writers elsewhere charge for such services, and use this as a starting point in your negotiations. I always get 50 percent of the fee upfront from private business clients, having learned this tends to curtail later problems with receiving full payment. Unlike magazines, most businesses are used to paying advances for a wide range of services and seldom balk at the prospect. The prime advantage to receiving an advance is that you have money in your pocket while you are doing the work, so you can cover ongoing expenses without having to dip into a personal line of credit or other financing source.

Beyond corporate and government work are a host of other opportunities. Once you have done some magazine writing and worked in other related fields, consider approaching your local community adult-education facility to offer writing workshops in your areas of expertise. I have taught courses in magazine writing, novel writing, introductory creative writing, business writing, suspense writing, and science fiction and fantasy over many years, throughout the Okanagan valley. Louise's "Magazine Writing from the Boonies" one-day workshop has toured the interior of British Columbia and points in Washington State.

Watch also for opportunities to bid on local-history book projects organized by museums and historical societies. Many clubs and local companies also commission histories of their operations for significant anniversaries, such as their twenty-fifth or fiftieth year in their area.

As your profile in the community grows, people may come to you for ghostwriting, manuscript reading, and proofing work. If you take on such work, be professional, objective, and thorough in making their efforts as publishable as possible. Resist the temptation to give them merely what you think they want. Novice writers may not appreciate paying you $200 to review the novel of their dreams, only to be told that the book is unpublishable, the writing amateurish, and the plot as thin as spring ice; but they are better off learning it now rather than after they've spent hundreds of dollars trying to market something that will never sell.

Finally, between innumerable writing assignments taken strictly for the money, you may find yourself wanting to try other writing forms. Don't hesitate to embark on the novel you have always wanted to write, or the non-fiction book that has been in the back of your mind for years, or the filmscript you think will take Hollywood by storm. The beauty of writing for a living is the sheer variety of options open to you. Reach out and try as many writing forms as you possibly can. Some will not be for you. Others may lead you down a path of creativity you never dreamed you'd follow. For a writer, there is always the chance to realize even the most challenging dream. Be daring. Trust yourself. Grab the creative moments that come your way and run with them as far as you can.

Dream on. And prosper.

CHAPTER
NINE

The Cheque Is Where?

Writing is a creative endeavour. So why a chapter devoted to ledgers, records, and bookkeeping? To keep the income-tax people happy, for one thing. More importantly, though, to make sure we get all our money. Logging postage expenses may not be your idea of a good time. On the other hand, you don't want to lose a hefty fee because you neglected to bill the magazine. However creative, magazine writing is a business. And good business requires good records.

The Paper Trail

Keeping good records is as simple as jotting your expenses and income in a scribbler. I use a two-column account journal available at any office-supply or drug store. I record all my purchases and fees, listing expenses in one column and income in the other. Like this:

Date		Description	Expenses	Income
Apr	3	Canada Post/postage	4.20	
	10	Bookland/magazines	7.50	
	12	RD Office Supplies/paper	43.75	
	15	*Chef Mag*/Purple Plum story		500.00
	16	BC Tel Long-distance calls	58.40	
	28	*Chef Mag*/Plum expenses		35.90

Record expenses (postage, paper, etc.) as they occur. (If you are registered with Revenue Canada, you may wish to add two more columns — one to track the GST you pay on purchases and the other to list the GST you bill magazines.) List income on the date you receive the cheques. In this hypothetical example, I received a cheque from *Chef Magazine* on April 15. The next day, my telephone bill arrived and I calculated the long-distance expenses pertaining to writing (including calls for research on both sold and unsold stories). They came to $58.40. I billed *Chef Magazine* for the calls relating to their Purple Plum story and received a cheque for $35.90 on April 28.

In my workshop, there's always some confusion over recording expenses, such as long-distance calls, for which you will later be reimbursed. In my example, I had $58.40 in long distance expenses of which $35.90 was charged to *Chef Magazine* and eventually received. That leaves $22.50 owing. This could be for a story for another magazine I've yet to bill. Or it could be for research on a story I never manage to sell. If the latter turns out to be the case, the $22.50 will remain as an expense. So I find the best method is to record all expenses and then record any reimbursements as income. This works. Trust me.

In the back of my account journal, I also record the date I submit (and invoice for) a manuscript. When I receive a cheque from a magazine, I tick off the appropriate listing. I check this page every now and then and issue follow-up invoices for any late payments. It's hard to imagine not noticing that you haven't been paid for a story (especially in the beginning, when we wait so anxiously for our cheques), but it can happen during a busy streak. Some type of "record of accounts receivable" prevents this calamity.

I also keep a telephone log of my writing-related long-distance calls. In a notepad by my phone I record the date, name, telephone number, and story each call pertains to. When I get my telephone bill, I highlight all the calls listed in my log. If I have calls for three stories, I make three photocopies of my bill and file them. This includes story ideas I'm researching but haven't yet sold. When I'm ready to invoice a magazine for a particular story, I have a copy of my phone bill on hand. I find this easier than digging out my bills later and determining which calls were for which story.

I keep another notepad in my car glovebox to record my mileage when I'm driving for business — to an interview, the library, the post office. I also record my odometer reading when I fill my car with gas. Later, I explain how to use these figures to calculate your automobile expenses.

The last record book I keep is a scribbler where I record all my submissions and correspondence. I can look up how many queries I've sent in the last few months, when I mailed a given manuscript, or from whom I requested research material. I note calls and assignments from editors on my calendar.

I enjoy maintaining these four books on a daily basis. It gives me a sense of productivity. Mark, however, derives absolutely no pleasure from a neatly tabulated column of figures. His attitude towards bookkeeping is hostile, to say the least, but he perseveres. He prefers to log his figures in a day-book and tackles his paperwork in periodic bursts. Still, he maintains accurate records that allow him to run his business efficiently.

Develop a system that works for you and keep it up to date. No one says you have to like it.

Can I Claim This?

A more palatable topic is deductible expenses. If you write with the intention of generating an income, as opposed to writing for a hobby, you can deduct related expenses from your earnings. This is where keeping good books comes in. Your submission log (with copies of your query letters) proves you actively market your work. Your account journal, along with original receipts (not cancelled cheques) provides an accurate record of your business expenses.

This book is a legitimate expense. So are other writing books, magazines, workshops, and a certain number (usually two per year) of writers' conventions. Office supplies, advertising, dues for writing associations, and office and travel costs are expenses too. Meals and entertainment, with certain restrictions, qualify. As does any expense resulting from pursuing writing as a business.

Consumable items, like office supplies, are written off in the year they're purchased. Items with a lasting value, such as your computer or your car, are depreciated over a certain number of years. This means you write off a percentage of their initial purchase price each year.

I record most expenses as they occur, but there are two I find easier to calculate at the end of the year: car expenses and the costs of running my office. I save all my receipts for gas, oil changes, new tires, and car insurance in a file and then add them up at the end of the year. I use my car for purposes other than writing so I can't claim the entire amount. My mileage log makes it easy to figure out the percentage of car expenses I use for business. My recorded odometer readings tell me the distance I've driven in a year. The mileage log tells me how much of that distance was for business. If it works out to, say, 50 percent, then I claim 50 percent of my total car expenses.

You can calculate office costs with a similar method. If you use one room in an eight-room house, then you generally deduct one-eighth of utility, insurance, property tax, and mortgage interest costs. Alternatively, you can work out the square footage your office occupies as a percentage of your home's total size.

These bookkeeping and income-tax tips are general guidelines only. This very basic advice is probably sufficient when you're starting out. As you progress in your career, it may be advantageous to consult an accountant. Meanwhile, contact your local taxation office for more specific information, including details on the Goods and Services Tax mentioned in Chapter Seven.

File and Smile

Magazine writers also need to maintain a good filing system. Not only do you need to organize current projects but you require some place to store published work for re-marketing and research material for future articles.

I still save all the ten-by-thirteen-inch envelopes from my junk mail. Slit lengthwise, they make economical files. And they hold papers more securely than file folders which are open on the sides. When I start a project, I label one of these envelopes and then use it to file every scrap of related material — notes, interview transcripts, research papers. On the outside of the envelope I list all contacts and their addresses and phone numbers. I also tuck in a copy of the article when it's published (usually the complete magazine), photos, and any correspondence the article generates. Perhaps a fan letter from a reader who found your article informative and entertaining. (Thanks, Mom.)

Keep copies of everything — your manuscript, cutlines, fact-checker list, invoices, letters — in your file. When editors call to suggest changes, it's usually quicker to pull out a paper copy of your manuscript than to call it up on your computer. Also, things get lost at magazine offices. You may get a frantic call saying your cutlines have been misplaced. If you have a copy handy, you can read them right over the phone.

Even after the article is published, I continue to add new information to its file. Blended with some of my old material, it might spin off into a new story. Or it might suggest markets for lucrative reprint rights.

Keep adding to your idea files, too. A newspaper filler, a brochure, or an advertisement can trigger a story idea. Often this initial information is too lean to query on, but with additional clippings and research, the file can grow into a potential article. For quite awhile, I've been collecting data on the proliferation of financial services for children, including a bank for kids only. One day, it should gel into a dynamite query.

I also keep copies of my best articles in a leather portfolio. It makes a good presentation at my workshops and it's an effective way to reassure interview subjects. If they're hesitant to talk to me, flipping through my previous work usually puts them at ease.

Be Nice

I pack my portfolio along when I speak to writers' organizations or represent the writing profession at events like career fairs. I like public speaking; it's a wonderful antidote to the isolation of writing. Even if I didn't, though, I would make the effort. It's good for business. The more you are recognized as a writer, the more writing opportunities — often very profitable ones like public-relations work or copy writing — come your way. As Mark mentioned, if you want to write for a living, take the jobs that come along so that, eventually, you can devote your time to the writing you most enjoy.

Send thank-you notes to your interview subjects and your major contacts. I like to wait until the article is published and then send along a copy. Often the larger magazines do this for you. Nice promotes success.

Be Tough

There may come a time, unfortunately, when you have to get tough, perhaps even downright nasty. And that's over late payments. This is rare, if you don't count the annoying policy of payment on publication, or the accounting procedures that mean even the good magazines delay your cheques for thirty days. I'm talking about magazines that hold up payment for months or have no intention of ever issuing a cheque.

This has only happened to me once and the odd time to Mark. We both found that the best solution is polite, but constant, demands for payment. Shortly after the time you expected payment has passed, send out another invoice clearly marked, "Second request for payment." Some writers add a late-payment charge. Follow up with a letter asking the editor to look into the matter. Then, assuming this doesn't work, write stronger letters. Phone calls at this point can be effective. Try calling collect. Although the magazine I was dealing with refused to pay me, they still, oddly, accepted my collect calls. After you've exhausted all means available to you, you may have to turn the matter over to the grievance committee of your professional writers group. In all fairness, they can only help if you have a signed contract. Your last alternative is to seek legal advice or take legal action on your own. You must decide whether the cost and time involved make this worthwhile.

In Chapter Three, I said I'd never been stung. I came close with this one case of non-payment; however, after innumerable phone calls and letters to the magazine, I eventually received a cheque. I won, so it wasn't an entirely bleak experience, but one I hope remains unique in my writing career. Needless to say, I didn't write for that magazine again. Next, Mark covers other problems you can encounter and the many, many good things magazine writing offers.

CHAPTER TEN

The Writing Life

Where do you get the stamp of government approval certifying you as an accredited professional writer? There ain't no such thing. None of the creative-writing degrees and journalism courses you take will ever confirm you as a writer. The only route to becoming a recognized professional is through publishing. If you want to call yourself a writer, you must publish. And you must keep publishing or you will have to start saying, "I used to be a writer, ..." Even corporate writers, who are often among the most professional of us, publish material, whether contributions to annual reports, the speeches of the company president, or advertising copy. All writers produce words that find their way into print, film, computer data-bases, or radio shows. So, if you want to be a writer, write. There is no other way.

It doesn't even matter how much money you earn annually. You don't have to prove a certain level of income to be accepted into the fold. Money is important to writers. Spend an hour with four writers and you hear more discussion of rates and how to make greater amounts of money than talk of postmodern literary deconstructivism. In the end, though, how much money you need to be a writer depends on how much you need to sustain the quality of life you want.

There is a lovely element of anarchism in being a writer. You are free to set your own goals, write about whatever you wish, earn however much you need for minimal survival, and only punch the clock when you want. Freedom like this is to be savoured. But such freedom forces upon you a great deal of responsibility: the responsibility for yourself.

If you fail as a writer, you have only yourself to blame. You can't blame the company boss, the union, the government, the ups and downs of the economy, or even your parents for never understanding you. When you decide to become a writer, particularly a boonie writer of magazine articles, you decide to stand alone. I think this is a brave stance. And I admire the courage of every writer I know who is working freelance, myself included.

The word freelance emerged in the Middle Ages when it was used to denote a knight who offered up the services of his lance for hire to feudal lords. Freelance writers do well to remember the origin of the word because it clearly defines their way of living. We must earn money to live; so, like the freelance knights, we do our best to get the most money for our efforts. This is an essential part of being a professional in any field of endeavour.

And if we want to succeed as writers, we also use our freedom of creative pursuit to best advantage. That means working hard at our craft. Professional writers write. They don't play golf every day, crochet in front of their keyboard, have the cleanest house on the block, or the deepest summer tan. Asked what they do for a living, they don't reply, "Well, I, ah, I work on my tan and in between I write a bit."

If you want to be a professional writer you must, like any professional, discipline yourself. You must spend time learning and studying your craft and keep abreast of developments in the creative industries that affect you. You must work hard to chase down markets and sell your writing. And you must, absolutely must, write; spending long, hard hours at the keyboard, or scribbling into your notepad, or whatever tool of expression you find best. That is the only way you ever produce the words that allow you to publish the material that justifies your title of "writer".

Okay, end of lecture. You get the drift. Just remember this when the sun is beating into your office and you imagine yourself floating in a cool body of water rather than hunkering sweatily over your keyboard. The writer stays. The floater heads for the beach. The choice is yours.

Doing Right: The Ethical Writer

Throughout your career as a writer you continually face a wide range of ethical problems. And how you decide to act on these problems moulds your perception of yourself as a writer and determines how others, inside and outside the business, perceive you.

Earlier I compared the writer to the freelance knight of old, and the analogy applies well when it comes to ethical considerations. There were many different types of freelance knights in the Middle Ages. Some fought for anyone against anyone; their only guide was the weight of the coin paid. Others looked upon knighthood as a profession governed by an honourable code of chivalrous behaviour where might was not always right, and the coin offered for services was accepted only if the cause was just.

As a writer, you too must weigh rightness of cause against the weight of coin offered. And no matter how honourable you think you are, the decision to walk away from work is among the hardest you will ever make.

I am pretty mercenary in the kinds of writing I undertake. Some of my colleagues refuse, as a matter of course, to write advertorials (advertising features thinly disguised as feature articles), promotional material, or articles on subjects that do not inspire them. I feel few boonie writers can afford this luxury and usually take any work that pays well.

Yet even I draw lines beyond which I won't step. You, too, have to establish lines for yourself. In some cases these lines are self-evident. Few writers contribute to a publication they find morally repugnant. That, of course, is a subjective decision, based on personal values. One writer might not write for an anti-abortion magazine. Another might refuse to work for *Penthouse*.

Often, however, the question is more subtle. A newsmagazine wants a quick story on the grief of a woman who has just watched her daughter and grandchildren gunned down by the daughter's husband, outside the neighbourhood recreation centre. They want the shock appeal only and really couldn't care less about the long-term consequences, whether the killer is brought to justice, or any significant aspect of the story. They want blood, horror, and cries for vengeance. Do you write the story? Again, the decision is yours. I did. In retrospect, I wish I hadn't. I no longer do these kinds of stories unless I feel I can go deeply enough into the material to draw some meaningful truth from the tragedy. I do not feel the writer's role is to produce pure sensationalism from the misery of others. You might feel differently and you are free to choose, as a freelance writer.

Not all ethical questions are as weighted with moral overtones as this. Most often, they concern the nature of establishing a professional relationship with your editors and the subjects of articles.

You owe it to your subjects to do the very best you can at telling their story truthfully and clearly. This means you must neither twist the truth to cast them in a bad light, nor embellish it to make them seem better than they are. Your job as a magazine writer is to seek the truth and reveal it in a piece of vivid writing. Sometimes the writing could be more vivid, more compelling, if you just added an imagined detail here, or subtracted a factual element there. Resist the urge. Stay faithful to yourself as a writer by stating the facts.

Also, be careful not to delude your subjects by winning your way into their confidence through offers of false friendship. In Chapter Five, Louise mentioned ways to get people to open up during interviews, and I described how a little covert spying could enhance your research base. That is all fair game. It is what journalists of all persuasions do as part of their craft (some would say, craftiness). But you should never step beyond these techniques to the point where subjects forget that everything they say can and will be used against them. Be professional with your subjects. Usually, this means retaining a courteous distance so that they remember you are there to tell their story, not to be their friend.

You are also not there to raid their files when they have their backs turned, or pull any of the other tricks you may have seen Humphrey Bogart doing in a late-night movie. If

something is in plain view, you can take a peek if the opportunity arises. But when subjects leave the room, resist the
urge to rummage through their drawers, flip through their
appointment book, or see what they hide in their bathroom
cabinet. Just as you would respect the privacy of family and
friends, show the same courtesy to your subjects.

Often, you find yourself faced with another dilemma. You
have just drawn a juicy quote from someone, who then says
something like, "By the way, you can't use any of that." I
have a stock response for this. I say, "Sorry, that's not how
it's done. If you wanted the material off the record you should
have said so before we started and I could then either have
agreed to those terms or terminated the interview." This is,
by the way, the standard rule among most major newspapers
in North America, so it is not arbitrary.

Sometimes, if I am dealing with someone who is clearly
a novice when it comes to interviews, and we seem to be
straying into some controversial area of discussion, I interrupt
and point out that everything we are talking about is going
to be used, with their name attached. If they back up at that
point, fine; but if they proceed, then I use the material.

Most people you interview have probably been around the
interview circuit a bit and can fend for themselves. Politi-
cians, civil servants, businessmen, religious proponents, ce-
lebrities, social activists, and Native leaders are examples of
this group. The woman on welfare who starts telling you
about how she tends bar on the side once a month to earn a
little extra is an example of the other end of the spectrum.
Which just goes to show that journalistic ethics aren't always
equivalent to the rights and wrongs of the legal system.

If someone you are interviewing states the material is going
to be off the record, or is not for attribution (meaning you can
use the material but not name the source), decide: Is there
anything to be gained in the way of background information
by proceeding? Could you get the same information on the
record from another source? Do you want to hear what your
subject is offering if you can't use it? If you proceed with the
interview, you are bound by your agreement, whether it's not

to use the material, or not to cite your subject as the source of the material.

When one source says something controversial about another person, you should in fairness give that person the opportunity to respond in the article to the allegation. This is true even of unattributed source material. If someone says, "On December 25, 1992, Bill Jones terrorized his neighbours by putting on a red suit and a white beard and climbing down their chimneys," you have to call Bill Jones and ask him whether it is true. You then include in the story his response. "It's a lie. The beard's black. I can't get the soot out."

Your sources are your responsibility. If you use unrevealed sources to piece a story together, you are expected by your peers to protect those sources against all comers. That includes police, courts, and heavies with large clubs who accost you in darkened back alleys, or men in mismatched plaid sportscoats offering wonderful sums of money for names. More than one journalist has gone to jail for contempt of court after refusing to surrender the names of people who revealed government secrets to them. Some of these journalists have been Canadians writing in this country. It is something that could happen to you, if you agree to take information without quoting the source. Still, if you let the quote pass, you might lose a story that sets a government on its head. Any story like this is a good story, the kind that makes writers' reputations grow and their rates for articles rise.

Just as you have to be ethical with subjects, so you must be in your dealings with editors. Let's start with boundaries in the relationship between writers and editors. I have a few editors I call friends — a very few. These are people I have worked with for many years, people I respect and about whose private lives I have come to know a good deal, through hours spent on the phone and the occasional visit; they know more about me, too, than most editors ever will or will want to. And these friendships can be difficult. In almost all of them there have been times when we have had to stand up against each other, so that the friendship has suddenly been jeopardized. There is a temptation on the part of many, often lonely, boonie writers to want to be friends with every editor they work with. Resist the urge. Be professional, polite, courteous, make a few jokes, even; but always remember you are engaged in a business relationship with this person, and the old maxim that relatives and friends make poor business partners can be particularly true in the writing industry.

There will come times when ethical dilemmas will arise between you and your editor. It is inevitable. Louise and I have mentioned several examples in other parts of this book. The most important thing you can do to prevent ethical entanglements is to be as good a writer and researcher as possible. Never show the completed article to sources without the prior permission of your editor. If you make a serious error, and you are likely to do so at some point, don't try and dodge the responsibility or pass the buck. Take the blame and learn from the experience.

That said, don't accept the blame for mistakes generated by your editors or the magazine publisher. If you feel they are behaving unprofessionally, say so. Otherwise you are giving tacit approval to their behaviour. What unprofessional behaviour is likely to force you to stand up to your editor? Obviously, anything that jeopardizes your sources, or makes something in your article untrue. These are the areas where most problems arise.

But there is another area that can cause problems. When a writer submits a query to a magazine, most publications treat it as a statement of entitlement regarding the subject. If they are already working on an article related to that subject, most magazines immediately contact the writer and advise him of this fact. If, however, they have nothing related on the go, it is commonly assumed the writer now has a claim and should be involved in some way in the writing of the article.

If magazine editors feel a particular writer has insufficient ability or is not well positioned to write the article, they usually offer to pay a finder's fee to that writer. Acceptance of

the fee releases the magazine from the unwritten moral commitment to honour the writer's claim on the subject matter.
If the writers don't accept the fee and the editors still won't
assign the article to them, an ethical editor simply cancels
plans to write about the subject. I am speaking here, by
the way, of narrowly defined articles. Saying that you want
to write an article on pennystock trading is insufficient claim.
Saying that you want to write an article on winners and losers
who have traded on the pennystock exchange, with specific
names and circumstances, is a story proposal concrete enough
to establish a claim.

You may become embroiled in an ethical issue of this sort
if you receive an assignment offer from an editor to write an
article that infringes upon another writer's claim. If the editor doesn't tell you the idea came from another writer and
isn't paying that writer a finder's fee, you will probably write
the piece and be none the wiser. You haven't behaved uneth-
ically; the editor has, by using you as a dupe. But sometimes
the editor lets the cat out of the bag and tries to draw you
into collusion. When you know another writer proposed the
story and hasn't accepted a finder's fee as compensation, ask
yourself this: are ideas not the most marketable thing I have?
Would I want other writers stealing my ideas for their personal profit? If you don't like that idea, put yourself in the
other writer's shoes and refuse the assignment. Be sure to tell
the editor clearly and firmly why you are turning down the
work. You should also consider how safe your future ideas are
with that editor.

You're in a Heap of Trouble, Boy

There are many books on the subject of libel, and there isn't
room in this chapter or book to do justice to such a major
writing issue as this. But there are a few crucial points to
keep in mind to ensure that you never find yourself opening
up a court summons because of something you have written.

The first rule of thumb is simple. Never write anything you
don't know to be true. If someone makes a criminal allegation
against another person and you decide to write about it, do

whatever you can to corroborate the charge with concrete evidence that would hold up in a court of law. For that is precisely where you are likely to find yourself, defending the allegation. If someone says a senior minister of government uses prostitutes and pays for them with a government-issued credit card, you'd better have copies of the credit-card records from Night of Your Life Escorts bearing his signature, before taking this story to print. Otherwise, forget it, or turn your information over to the police and try to keep tabs of their investigation.

The same goes for statements that are not criminally related but might be construed as defamation of someone's character. You must be able to prove the truth of what you have written.

And don't think you needn't worry about libel on the grounds that no magazine is going to print something libellous. It happens, often without anyone realizing the material was contentious. And both you and the magazine will usually be sued. The problem is the editor is usually protected by the magazine's libel insurance; you probably are not. So be scrupulous in your research and don't be afraid to tell your editor if something comes up that seems controversial to you. If you feel strongly about it, ask that the magazine's lawyer approve the story, and if the editor refuses, request that your name be withdrawn from the article.

In the early months of 1991, a wind began blowing across Canada, referred to by writers as the Libel Chill. The wind had gathered in the cavernous towers of Toronto and Ottawa, where several powerful Canadians launched libel actions against writers who had expressed opinions on these people's behaviour. The law suits claimed defamation without showing any example of how the claimants had suffered any material, emotional, or image-related harm. The point is that under current Canadian libel legislation, the onus for proof rests on the writer. Claimants need not show they were libelled. It is up to the writer to show the claimant wasn't libelled and so can't be considered to have been harmed by the writing.

As I write, the Libel Chill still blows and many writers and magazine publishers are carefully refraining from writing anything openly critical of powerful Canadian figures, unless the evidence against them is entombed in concrete. But what is proof? If a senior government cabinet minister appears to have complete disregard for those supposedly served by that cabinet minister's mandate and you cite a few examples of that disregard, is that proof? Especially when they are examples of behaviour rather than written policy? This question is increasingly being answered in the courts. Only time and legal precedent will determine to what extent writers must self-censor their writing in order to avoid being touched by the damaging winds of the Libel Chill. But it is unlikely the result of these legal challenges will be a nation where the boundaries of freedom of expression are expanded.

Being Part of the Community

The decision to become a writer means that, wittingly or not, you have joined a special fraternity. You are a member of the writing community, whose links spread across the country and continent, and ultimately encompass the globe. When we come into contact with space-alien writers, they, too, will become part of this group who share a unique commonality.

A boonie writer's life can often seem lonely and isolating. Most freelance writers work from home offices, sometimes going days without the normal social contacts that are a daily part of nine-to-five jobs. Often, it is this very sense of isolation that leads many writers to give up the freelance life and find a day job with a magazine, newspaper, or corporation, or, eventually, to abandon writing altogether.

But being a writer does not have to be a totally solitary pursuit. Even if you are the only writer in your community, you are not alone. Scattered across the breadth of this land are hundreds of people doing precisely the same work as you. Some are fellow boonie writers. Others write from metropolitan home offices. No matter where they live, they share the same frustrations of finding the right image, pulling a precise word from their internal dictionary, or convincing a particular editor to have good sense, for a change. The more you learn about other writers, the more you realize that many problems you thought were uniquely yours are common to all of us.

To break down the walls of isolation in the writing life, consider participating in the larger writing community by attending writing conferences, establishing friendships with other writers, and joining writers' associations. No matter what kind of writing you are involved in, there is an association for your particular interest.

Many communities, even those with populations of only a few thousand, have local writing groups (often affiliated with the Canadian Authors Association or a similar body) that meet regularly for educational sessions and general chit-chat. You may find becoming involved in such a group provides that social outlet you miss as a writer working in the isolation of home.

At the national and provincial levels there are numerous associations to choose from. For magazine writers, the one most immediately involved in our field is the Periodical Writers Association of Canada. If you specialize in magazine writing on specific topics like health issues or outdoor subjects, membership in associations for science writers or outdoor writers might also be useful.

Most of these associations publish regular newsletters updating markets and sharing new writing techniques and profitable sales tactics. They usually hold at least one annual conference a year for their membership. For the past few years, I have regularly attended the PWAC annual general meeting held in various locations across the country. As a result, I have met and come to know writers working from such places as an outport on the coast of Labrador, a cabin verging on the tundra in the Northwest Territories, to a lovely 1930s vintage apartment in the heart of Montreal. Friendships have resulted from these meetings that are every bit as valuable as the professional knowledge I have gleaned from some of the most experienced people in the magazine industry.

The same thing happens at writing conferences. Besides being exposed to a wealth of advice offered during the courses

and speaking sessions, you meet many fellow writers. Friendships develop, relationships often maintained by little more
than the occasional letter. But they are special friendships
founded on the common bond you share by being engaged in
a profession that is as much a way of life as a business pursuit.

Writing sparks a way of looking at the world that sets you
apart from people who are not engaged in similar creative
pursuits. This happens whether you want it to or not. It
doesn't mean you are better than others, or brighter, or even
more deranged; it simply means you are different.

The reason for this is that writers can never truly step back
from their work and be done with it for a day, or a two-week
vacation, or a year-long sabbatical. This doesn't mean you
are a workaholic. Rather, you are engaged in a pursuit that
draws on most areas of your mind. And when you step back
from the keyboard at day's end, you can't simply shut down
the creative aspect of your mind, even if you believe you do.
You may refuse to listen to what it is telling you, but it goes
on developing, creating, and looking at the world with an eye
to what you can use in your writing.

So while you are ironing clothes, mowing the lawn, listen-
ing to your stockbroker's latest bad investment advice, or
grinding spices to make Chicken Creole, you are often only
partially engaged in the activity at hand. The writer in you
is off somewhere entirely different, piecing together the facts
in the way you really wanted to write the article before but
couldn't. Or noticing how the stockbroker's tie is dotted with
dried egg yoke and recalling how the person you interviewed
yesterday had the same stains, which you forgot to mention in
your descriptive passage, although the stains were as telling
as the dirty fingernails you did mention, and the image would
be much stronger if you linked the two.

Non-writing friends and family start noticing how often
your eyes seem to lose focus when they talk to you, and how
you seem to withdraw to somewhere outside the conversation.
As time goes on, they learn to recognize you have merely
kicked into full writer gear and will be back soon enough if
they don't pester you. Most come to respect these instances

for the valuable creative moments they are. A few resent that something besides themselves can hold such powerful sway over you; but do not give into them by suppressing your creativity. Be true to yourself as a writer and you cannot go too far wrong. It is down that road that a writer finds the greatest fulfilment in life.

Having embarked as a writer, you, like Robert Frost, are setting off on a road less travelled. And like him, if you stick with it, you find the decision to follow that poorly marked pathway makes all the difference. May your journey be wonderful.

EPILOGUE

Good Luck but Not Goodbye

Writing is lonely. It's a solitary craft; just you and a blank page or computer screen. If you live in the boonies, where writers are often rare, it's even more isolating. Only another writer understands the joy of hammering out a knock-out lead, pulling off a dynamite interview, or landing a big story. And only another writer appreciates the energy required to market relentlessly, to handle rejection, and to continue writing.

Talking to you has been a marvellous opportunity for Mark and me to remedy our own isolation out here in British Columbia's beautiful, but often writer-thin, Okanagan Valley, and we want to share one last bit of encouragement.

Non-fiction magazine articles are the quickest way to become published. There is a magazine dedicated to virtually every subject imaginable — from news to nuts, fashion to farming, sports to sprockets — making this the easiest field to break into. You are bound to discover at least one publication, and likely more, for your story idea. And as you've read, many magazines, especially trade journals, are looking for regional coverage. Editors want stories from your hometown. Contact them with a strong query letter and you're on your way. There's nothing like knowing that an editor wants your story to spur you to write your best.

If you want to write and be published no matter where you live, Mark and I hope this book is the gentle nudge you need. We want our experiences — Mark's as an established pro with regular assignments and mine as a relative newcomer — to banish any doubts about writing from the boonies. Use our guidelines to get started, but trust your own judgement. Our best advice is to take any writing book, ours included, with a grain of salt. It's your unique perspective on the world that makes you a marketable writer and your own determination that guarantees success.

It's been a pleasure talking to you and we'd love to hear from you. Drop us a line at the following address and, if you'd like a reply, enclose a SASE. Good luck and good writing.

Best wishes.

Mark Zuehlke and Louise Donnelly
c/o Carleton University Press Inc.
160 Paterson Hall
Carleton University
Ottawa Ontario K1S 5B6

Useful Books and Services

Over the years, we have found the following eclectic mix of books helpful in our magazine writing from the boonies.

Writing Basics

Baker, Sheridan. *The Practical Stylist, Canadian Edition*. New York: Harper & Row, Publishers, Inc., 1983. An excellent detailed guide covering grammar basics from punctuation to sentence and paragraph structure.

Gordon, Karen Elizabeth. *The Transitive Vampire: A Handbook of Grammar for the Innocent, the Eager, and the Doomed*. New York: Times Books, 1984. An entertaining and even titillating guide to grammar, with seductive examples.

———. *The Well-Tempered Sentence: A Punctuation Handbook for the Innocent, the Eager, and the Doomed*. New York: Ticknor & Fields, 1983. A provocative sample-filled guide for those who learn best from example rather than explanation.

University of Chicago. *A Manual of Style*. Chicago: University of Chicago Press, 1969. Expensive, but the most thorough guide to manuscript preparation, editing methods, and proofreaders' marks with an answer to virtually any question on writing basics.

White, E.B., and William Strunk Jr. *The Elements of Style*. New York: Macmillan Publishing Co., Inc., 1979. Remains the most readable and condensed guide to elementary rules of usage and composition.

Magazine Writing

Drobot, Eve, and Hal Tennant, eds. *Words for Sale*. Toronto: Macmillan of Canada, 1990. A guide to writing for Canadian magazines, written by members of the Periodical Writers Association of Canada. Covers most basics.

Hubbard, J.T.W. *Magazine Editing: How to Acquire the Skills You Need to Win a Job and Succeed in the Magazine Business*. Syracuse, NY: Syracuse University Press, 1988. Excellent book for writers *and* editors with eminently practical tips on leads and profiles.

Nonfiction, Style and Technique

Cheney, Theodore A. *Writing Creative Nonfiction*. Cincinnati, OH: Writer's Digest Books, 1987. Shows how to transform prose on any subject into dramatically effective writing.

Klauser, Henriette Anne. *Writing On Both Sides of the Brain*. New York: HarperCollins, 1987. Techniques for productivity, freeing creativity and honing editing skills.

Zinsser, William. *On Writing Well: An Informal Guide to Writing Nonfiction*. 2nd ed. New York: Harper & Row Publishers, Inc., 1980. Highly readable guide to better writing. A must buy.

Magazine Production

Bruno, Michael. *Pocket Pal: A Graphic Arts Production Handbook*. 13th ed. Memphis, TN: International Paper Company, 1988. First printed in 1934. Takes you in detail through every aspect of the printing process from inks, to photo-overlay methods, to printing press variations.

Mogel, Leonard. *The Magazine: Everything You Need to Know to Make it in the Magazine Business*. Chester, CT: Globe Pequot Press, 1988. An insider's look at the industry.

Rogers, Geoffrey. *Editing for Print*. London: Quarto Publishing Ltd. 1985. A reference book written for editors that covers every procedure involved in the book, magazine, and editing/production process.

Market Directories

Canadian Magazines For Everyone. Toronto: Canadian Magazine Publishers Association. While this annual catalogue of members' publications does not provide information for writers, it's useful for editorial descriptions of many magazines not available in the boonies. Request price for catalogue from 2 Stewart Street, Toronto, M5V 1H6.

Canadian Markets for Writers and Photographers. Edmonton, AB: Proof Positive. The most complete market guide for Canada. Available at bookstores or by phoning 1-800-361-2349.

Literary Market Place. New Providence, NJ: Reed Publishing (USA) Inc. A hefty annual directory, with contacts, to the North American publishing industry.

Writer's Market. Cincinnati, OH: Writer's Digest Books. An annual publication listing four thousand publishers and magazine markets. Some Canadian listings but most useful for breaking into the American market. (This same publisher also brings out annual market guides for fiction and other writing fields.)

Freelancing

Hanson, Nancy Edmonds. *How You Can Make $25,000 a Year Writing (No Matter Where You Live)*. Cincinnati, OH: Writer's Digest Books, 1987. Advice for those already in the writing business who are thinking of going it alone.

Whittlesey, Marietta. *Freelance Forever: Successful Self-Employment*. New York: Avon Books, 1982. A complete directory on how to make it on your own no matter what profession you are involved in.

Interviews

Schumacher, Michael. *Creative Conversations: The Writer's Complete Guide to Conducting Interviews*. Cincinnati, OH: Writer's Digest Books, 1990. Nuts-and-bolts advice with anecdotes.

Photography

Calder, Julian, and John Garrett. *The 35MM Photographer's Handbook*. London: Pan Books Ltd., 1979. Covers everything you could want to know about photography.

Patterson, Freeman. *Photography & the art of seeing*. Toronto: Van Nostrand Reinhold Ltd., 1979. An inspirational work by the famous Canadian photographer that shows how to transform your craftsmanlike photography into art.

Libel

Porter, Julian, Q.C. *Libel: A Handbook for Canadian Publishers, Editors and Writers*. Toronto: Canadian Book Publishers' Council, 1987. A question-and-answer guide available from the Writers' Union of Canada, in Toronto.

Research and Sources

Overbury, Steven. *Finding Canadian Facts Fast*. Toronto: Methuen, 1985. A professional researcher reveals how a skip tracer, private eye, librarian, and others track down information and contacts.

The following directories, usually found in the reference section of most libraries, list potential sources.

Annual Corpus Almanac & Canadian Sourcebook. Don Mills, Ontario: Southam Business Information & Communications. Published annually, this book lists statistics and leading experts in various fields.

Canadian Almanac & Directory. Toronto: Copp Clark Limted. An annual listing of data and contacts with addresses and phone numbers.

Directory of Associations in Canada. Toronto: Micromedia Limited. Published every two years, this guide provides contacts, including regional representatives, with addresses and phone numbers.

Sources: The Directory of Contacts for Editors, Reporters and Researchers. A general reference listing of experts and contacts, *Sources* is published twice a year and mailed free to bona fide journalistic personnel who write to Suite 109, 4 Phipps Street, Toronto, Ontario, M4Y 1J5.

We also have found these next services invaluable for sources and information.

Media Link. A free research service developed for the Canadian media. Writers call 1-800-387-4643 to request contacts in dozen of fields from real estate to agriculture.

Statistics Canada. Check your telephone directory for the toll-free number for the nearest office of this federal-government department. A friendly and helpful staff provide statistical data on innumerable topics.

Beyond Magazines: Other Writing Forms

Bivins, Thomas. *Handbook for Public Relations Writing.* Lincolnwood, IL: National Textbook Company, 1989. Covers in detail almost every form of corporate and public-relations writing, from press releases, to brochures, to promotional films.

Hauge, Michael. *Writing Screenplays that Sell.* New York: Harper-Collins Publishers, 1991. Easily understood, thorough guide to writing in a challenging but lucrative field.

Koontz, Dean R. *How to Write Best Selling Fiction.* Cincinnati, OH: Writer's Digest Books, 1981. An excellent guide to writing commercial fiction that focuses on producing marketable fiction rather than art.

Surmelian, Leon. *Techniques of Fiction Writing: Measure and Madness.* New York: Doubleday & Company, Inc., 1969. Densely written treatment of fiction-writing techniques, loaded with rich examples.

The Writing Life

Brohaugh, William, ed. *Just Open A Vein.* Cincinnati, OH: Writer's Digest Books, 1987. A host of writers on the joys, pains, and requirements of living the writer's life.

Gardner, John. *On Becoming A Novelist.* New York: Harper & Row, Publishers, Inc., 1983. The late novelist and teacher's thoughts on what it takes to be a novelist and to succeed at the business.

Sternburg, Jane. *The Writer on Her Work.* New York: W.W. Norton & Company, 1980. Women writers like Anne Tyler discuss the origins of their work and the problems they face. An excellent read for male writers, as well.

Strickland, Bill. *On Being A Writer*. Cincinnati, OH: Writer's Digest Books, 1989. From Earnest Hemingway to Tom Robbins, some of the twentieth century's top writers talk about their work, lives, failures, and triumphs.

APPENDIX

Standard Freelance Publication Agreement

Approved by the Periodical Writers Association
of Canada

This agreement is between ⸺⸺⸺⸺⸺ (Writer)
and ⸺⸺⸺⸺⸺⸺ (Publication/Client)
Working Title: ⸺⸺⸺⸺⸺⸺⸺
Byline to read: ⸺⸺⸺⸺⸺⸺⸺
Source of idea (check one): Writer ⸺⸺ Publication ⸺⸺
Description of assignment:

Approximate length of article: ⸺⸺⸺⸺⸺
Deadline: ⸺⸺⸺⸺⸺⸺⸺⸺
Tentative publication date: ⸺⸺⸺⸺⸺⸺

Rights Licensed (check):
    First Canadian serial rights only
    ⸺⸺ English   ⸺⸺ French   ⸺⸺ Other:

Fee: $⸺⸺⸺⸺⸺⸺

Expenses: The Publication agrees to reimburse the Writer for direct expenses incurred in fulfilling this agreement. Such expenses include photocopying, fax, long-distance telephone calls, and couriers, ⸺⸺⸺ . Such expenses will not exceed a maximum amount of $⸺⸺⸺ .

Travel Expenses: The Publication agrees to reimburse the Writer for travel expenses to a maximum amount of $⸺⸺⸺ . Travel expenses will include:

The Writer agrees to write, and the Publication agrees to publish, a manuscript in accordance with the terms of this agreement. This agreement includes any attached and initialed sheets. The fee specified in this agreement does not include Goods and Services (GST) or other applicable national or provincial sales tax.

_____ Date _____
(Publication representative)
_____ Date _____
(Writer)

For a detailed list of fine print terms of this contract contact:

> Periodical Writers Association of Canada
> 54 Wolseley St., 3rd Floor
> Toronto, ON
> M5T 1A5
> E-mail: PWAC@cycor.ca

This contract reproduced with the kind permission of the Periodical Writers Association of Canada.

INDEX